Indiana Legal Research

Carolina Academic Press
Legal Research Series

Tenielle Fordyce-Ruff, Series Editor
Suzanne E. Rowe, Series Editor Emerita
❧

Arizona, Fourth Edition — Tamara S. Herrera
Arkansas, Second Edition — Coleen M. Barger, Cheryl L. Reinhart &
Cathy L. Underwood
California, Fourth Edition — Aimee Dudovitz, Sarah Laubach & Suzanne E. Rowe
Colorado, Second Edition — Robert Michael Linz
Connecticut, Second Edition — Anne Rajotte & Jessica Rubin
Federal, Second Edition — Mary Garvey Algero, Spencer L. Simons,
Suzanne E. Rowe, Scott Childs & Sarah E. Ricks
Florida, Fifth Edition — Barbara J. Busharis, Anne E. Mullins & Suzanne E. Rowe
Georgia, Second Edition — Margaret Butler & Thomas Striepe
Hawai'i — Victoria Szymczak, Cory Lenz & Roberta Woods
Idaho, Third Edition — Tenielle Fordyce-Ruff
Illinois, Second Edition — Mark E. Wojcik
Indiana — Ashley Ames Ahlbrand & Michelle Trumbo
Iowa, Third Edition — John D. Edwards, Karen L. Wallace & Melissa H. Weresh
Kansas — Joseph A. Custer & Christopher L. Steadham
Kentucky, Second Edition — William A. Hilyerd, Kurt X. Metzmeier & David J. Ensign
Louisiana, Fourth Edition — Mary Garvey Algero
Massachusetts, Second Edition — E. Joan Blum & Shaun B. Spencer
Michigan, Fourth Edition — Cristina D. Lockwood
Minnesota — Suzanne Thorpe
Mississippi — Kristy L. Gilliland
Missouri, Fourth Edition — Wanda M. Temm & Julie M. Cheslik
New York, Fourth Edition — Elizabeth G. Adelman, Courtney L. Selby,
Brian Detweiler & Kathleen Darvil
North Carolina, Third Edition — Brenda D. Gibson, Julie L. Kimbrough,
Laura P. Graham & Nichelle J. Perry
North Dakota — Anne E. Mullins & Tammy Pettinato Oltz
Ohio, Second Edition — Sara Sampson, Katherine L. Hall & Carolyn Broering-Jacobs
Oklahoma — Darin K. Fox, Darla W. Jackson & Courtney L. Selby
Oregon, Fifth Edition — Suzanne E. Rowe & Megan Austin
Pennsylvania, Second Edition — Barbara J. Busharis, Catherine M. Dunn,
Bonny L. Tavares & Carla P. Wale
Tennessee, Second Edition — Scott Childs, Sibyl Marshall & Carol McCrehan Parker
Texas, Second Edition — Spencer L. Simons
Washington, Second Edition — Julie A. Heintz-Cho, Tom Cobb & Mary A. Hotchkiss
West Virginia, Second Edition — Hollee Schwartz Temple
Wisconsin — Patricia Cervenka & Leslie Behroozi
Wyoming, Second Edition — Debora A. Person & Tawnya K. Plumb
❧

Indiana Legal Research

Ashley Ames Ahlbrand
Michelle Trumbo

Tenielle Fordyce-Ruff, Series Editor
Suzanne E. Rowe, Series Editor Emerita

Carolina Academic Press
Durham, North Carolina

Library of Congress Cataloging-in-Publication Data

Names: Ahlbrand, Ashley, author. | Trumbo, Michelle, author.
Title: Indiana legal research / Ashley Ames Ahlbrand, Michelle Trumbo.
  Description: Durham, North Carolina : Carolina Academic Press, 2022. |
  Series: Legal research series
Identifiers: LCCN 2022016033 (print) | LCCN 2022016034 (ebook) | ISBN
  9781531018214 (paperback) | ISBN 9781531018221 (ebook)
Classification: LCC KFI3075 .A46 2022 (print) | LCC KFI3075 (ebook) |
  DDC
  340.072/0772—dc23/eng/20220526
LC record available at https://lccn.loc.gov/2022016033
LC ebook record available at https://lccn.loc.gov/2022016034

Carolina Academic Press
700 Kent Street
Durham, North Carolina 27701
(919) 489-7486
www.cap-press.com

Printed in the United States of America.

Summary of Contents

Contents

List of Tables

Acknowledgments

Thanks are owed to many people for their help with this book.

To the entire Jerome Hall Law Library staff, past and present, for giving us our first opportunities in law librarianship. Thank you for being such wonderful and enthusiastic colleagues. Go Hoosiers!

To Suzanne, our first editor, Tenielle, our second and current editor, and everyone at Carolina Academic Press for their suggestions, support, and (infinite) patience.

—A.A. & M.T.

To my co-author, Michelle, for sticking with me on this project over many years, miles, and job changes.

To my parents, for their encouragement, support, and accountability through every draft.

—A.A.

To my co-author, Ashley, whose hard work and dedication made this book possible. Thank you for keeping me on track and moving forward.

To J.T., my husband, for his unfailing support and encouragement of all my projects.

—M.T.

Preface

Indiana Legal Research is written for every legal researcher, those with a legal background and those without, those who have been practicing law in Indiana for years, and those new to the state's laws and legal resources. This book seeks to introduce the reader to the processes and techniques for conducting efficient and effective legal research, with a focus on Indiana sources and brief analogy to their federal counterparts. The book provides advice for conducting both print and electronic legal research, highlighting the tools available in either approach, and identifying the advantages and disadvantages of each, and times in the research process when one approach might be more beneficial than the other. Those more experienced at Indiana legal research will benefit from the book's gathering of all Indiana legal resources into one text, including both print and electronic, subscription-based and free, with examples of how and when to use each in the research process. The chapters of this book focus on discrete types of law and legal resources, from statutes and legislation to cases and court rules to administrative and executive materials to secondary sources in law. Additional chapters explore strategies for conducting, processing, and organizing one's research, and appendixes at the end provide advice on legal citation and additional research sources on the state of Indiana.

It is the authors' goal that *Indiana Legal Research* will be a helpful resource for researchers throughout the state of Indiana and beyond, those with the advantage of proximity to a law library and those living in more remote areas. Legal research can be a daunting endeavor, but this book and others in this series seek to make the process more manageable and relatable, regardless of one's familiarity with law and the legal system.

Series Note

The Legal Research Series published by Carolina Academic Press includes many titles from states around the country. The goal of each book is to provide law students, practitioners, paralegals, college students, and laypeople with the essential elements of legal research in each state. Unlike more bibliographic texts, the Legal Research Series books seek to explain concisely both the sources of state law research and the process for conducting legal research effectively.

Indiana Legal Research

Chapter 1

Conducting Legal Research: Process and Preliminaries

I. State and Federal Legal Research: Similarities and Differences

You will find that the sources of law, the publication of law, and the research process are very similar at the federal and state levels. The key to successful research in any jurisdiction is to know the best jurisdiction-specific resources to consult. This book will emphasize resources and tips for conducting legal research in Indiana, with brief descriptions of federal legal research to draw parallels and highlight differences.

II. Getting Ready to Research— Initial Considerations

A. Legal Analysis

You should begin any legal research process by analyzing your research problem:

- Identify the jurisdiction(s) involved—state or federal?
- List the key facts and legal issues—this list will likely develop more as your research progresses, but it can be extremely helpful to come up with a preliminary list from the start to help you determine where to begin your research.

- Jot down keywords and phrases—these will be convenient when it comes time to craft your searches (electronic research) or look for relevant sections of a resource in its index (print research).

- Compose your research question—although it may seem elementary, having a research question to refer back to can help you stay on track during your research, when it is easy to go down rabbit holes of "what ifs?"

Analyzing your research problem can be the most challenging aspect of the research process. You should expect your research analysis to develop as your research progresses; you may find new keywords and phrases to search, identify new legal issues, or even realize that you need to collect more information in order to fully research your scenario. You do not have to be an expert in law to conduct legal research; you just have to know which resources to use to best answer your question.

B. Legal Authority

As with many disciplines, resources in legal research divide into two categories: primary sources and secondary sources. *Primary sources* are the law itself: constitutions, statutes, cases, regulations, executive orders, and proclamations. When conducting legal research, finding relevant primary sources is your greatest goal because they tell you what the law says about your legal question. *Secondary sources*, on the other hand, are everything else, that is, any resource that explains, describes, or analyzes the law. Secondary sources are an excellent place to begin your research because they provide background on the topic you are researching and will lead you to the key primary sources on that topic. Chapter 3 covers secondary sources in greater detail.

In addition to primary and secondary sources, you must be able to distinguish between mandatory (or binding) and persuasive authority. *Mandatory authority* refers to what sources a court would be bound to follow if that court were deciding your legal question. This is where identifying your applicable jurisdiction in your initial research analysis becomes important. In Indiana, examples of binding authority include Indiana statutes, Indiana regulations, and cases from the Indiana Supreme Court. The laws of another jurisdiction can be *persuasive authority*, meaning they are not binding, but may be used in research as evidence of how other jurisdictions' laws govern a particular legal scenario. An attorney might use persuasive authority in instances where she is dealing with a new issue of law in her jurisdiction; the attorney could use another state's laws as an example of how her state should act on this issue. Table 1-1 shows the relationship between primary and secondary sources and mandatory and persuasive authority; notice that primary sources can have mandatory or persuasive authority, but secondary sources can have only persuasive authority.

Table 1-1. Mandatory and Persuasive Authority in Indiana

	Primary Sources	Secondary Sources
Mandatory/ Binding Authority	Indiana cases Indiana statutes Indiana Constitution Indiana regulations	
Persuasive Authority	Ohio cases Illinois statutes Kentucky Constitution Michigan regulations	Any secondary source, such as a law encyclopedia, treatise, or law journal

There is one more wrinkle in the discussion of legal authority. With several different types of primary sources that are all mandatory authority, we must recognize another aspect to authority, the hierarchy of authority. A jurisdiction cannot have a constitutional provision, a statute, and a case that conflict on an issue of law. Therefore, constitutions are the highest form of authority in any jurisdiction, followed by statutes, then regulations. Finally, when a legal issue is not addressed by a constitutional provision, statute, or regulation, judges have the power to create law through judicial decisions; we refer to this judge-made law as *common law*.[1] Table 1-2 depicts the hierarchy of primary sources.

---

1. In reality, there is more depth to this hierarchy than just this simple statement. For instance, if a there is an Indiana statute on the books that addresses a legal issue in a case before the Indiana Supreme Court, but the attorneys in the case are arguing the constitutionality of that statute, the Indiana Supreme Court may find the statute invalid on constitutional grounds, and decide therefore not to follow the statute's edicts. But in the face of a constitutionally valid statute or regulation, the court will apply the law as it is, rather than creating its own common law.

Table 1-2. Hierarchy of Primary Sources within a Jurisdiction

Constitution

Statutes

Regulations

Cases

C. Legal Research Process

With all of these different types of authority and levels of hierarchy, it can seem overwhelming to begin a legal research project. There is no one "right" way to begin your research—it will depend on the question you are researching—but when you are new to legal research, or even as a seasoned researcher exploring an unfamiliar area of law, the following recommended steps, described at length in this section and depicted in Table 1-3, will help ensure an efficient and effective legal research experience. The steps listed here offer a quick and easy-to-remember guide; Chapter 2 will expand upon these steps in further detail.

Table 1-3. Recommended Steps in the Legal Research Process

Recommended Steps	Description
1. Preliminary research analysis	Identify your research question, relevant legal and factual issues, keywords, and jurisdiction.
2. Start with secondary sources	Use secondary sources to provide background and context for your legal research question.
3. Identify relevant primary sources	Allow the secondary sources to lead you to key primary sources that answer your legal research question.
4. Reach a satisfactory stopping point	It can be challenging to determine when you have found the appropriate primary sources to definitively answer your legal research question. Some tips are provided in subsection 4, below.

1. Conduct the Preliminary Research Analysis

Begin, as stated earlier, by documenting what you already know from analyzing the problem: legal and factual issues, jurisdiction, keywords and phrases, and your research question. This preliminary analysis will serve as an excellent foundation for beginning your research. As research progresses, you can expect this analysis to evolve as well, as new legal issues come to light, new keywords or legal terms of art surface, and your research question comes into greater focus. If you find that your initial research is bringing up too many results, most of which are beyond the scope of your question, consider revising your keyword list with more specific terms. If instead you find your initial research is bringing back no results, consider expanding your keyword list to include broader terms.

2. Get Acquainted with Your Research Topic Through Secondary Sources

In most cases, you should begin your research in secondary sources. These sources provide background and analysis of different areas of law and will direct you to the key primary sources on point. If you were struggling to identify specific keywords for your research in step 1, secondary sources are an excellent resource for generating precise keywords on discrete topics. Secondary sources vary in depth and authority; legal encyclopedias, for example, offer quick, shallow overviews of legal topics, while legal treatises offer much more in-depth analysis of broad areas of law. Chapter 3 will delve into a variety of secondary sources, their contents, and when to use specific types of secondary sources in legal research. You may find yourself returning to secondary sources during your research process as new legal questions arise.

3. Locate the Relevant Law

In any legal research project, you want to find what the law itself says about your legal issue. It is not enough to see what an expert wrote about your topic in a treatise or law review article; you must always find the primary sources yourself. Because of the hierarchy among primary sources, you will typically begin this leg of your research by seeing if any statutes apply to your legal issue. From there you will move into case law research to see what the courts have said, and you may look to regulations as well, if applicable. Before relying on the statutes and cases you have found, you also want to use a tool called a *citator* to ensure that your primary authority is still good law (e.g., Has the statute been amended? Has the case been overturned?). Citators are tools found on specialized legal research platforms and will be covered more fully in the chapter on citators, Chapter 7.

4. Knowing When to Stop

The age-old question in legal research is this: How do you know when you are done? There is no golden answer, but instead you must rely on common sense and instinct. Consider whether the same resources keep coming up over and over in your research, and whether you have any more unanswered questions. At an even more practical level, it is time to stop if you have run out of time to conduct your research! For this reason, learning to be an efficient researcher is just as critical as being an effective researcher. Answering the question of when to stop becomes easier with practice; for the time being, rely on your instincts.

III. Where Do We Go from Here?

The rest of this book is dedicated to legal research resources and strategy. Chapter 2 offers tips on conducting research in print and electronically and highlights different ways to approach a legal research question. Chapter 3 discusses prominent secondary sources for legal research, both Indiana-specific and non-jurisdictional. Chapters 4 through 8 highlight primary sources: Chapter 4 discusses constitutions and statutes; Chapter 5 discusses court structure and judicial opinions; Chapter 6 discusses case law research; Chapter 7 discusses citators; and Chapter 8 discusses administrative law. Chapter 9 discusses a specialized area of research, legislative history. Chapter 10 concludes with a deeper dive into legal research planning and documentation. Finally, appendixes at the end of this book include tips on legal citation, with examples from Indiana resources; and a selective bibliography of Indiana legal, statistical, and governmental resources.

Chapter 2

Tools and Techniques
for Legal Research

After receiving a research assignment, determining the jurisdiction to research in, identifying keywords and phrases, and drafting your research question as covered in Chapter 1, you must begin to conduct research. This chapter introduces the tools and techniques you can use to research as well as how to develop a research plan.

I. Print v. Electronic Research

Today's legal landscape is dominated by online resources. Print resources still play a role and, in some situations, are superior in terms of ease of use and effectiveness than their electronic counterparts. Familiarity with print resources will also help you use their electronic equivalents more effectively. Print has advantages. One of these is that it naturally provides context due to its physical properties and organization. In contrast, electronic research is much more disembodied. The structure of a resource is broken down to transform it into a digital format. For example, statutory research is often easier and quicker in print as the hierarchy and interaction between different statutory sections is more evident.

Conversely, search capabilities are more powerful in an electronic format. Full-text searching can easily help you find all instances of a term or phrase in thousands of pages of information; however, this approach has limitations. An example of this is the "synonym problem." It occurs when your search terminology doesn't match the language used in the case or statute, which causes them not to appear in your results set (e.g., you ran a search for "dog" and the statute uses "canine" instead and, as a result, the law is not retrieved in response to your query). As an alternative to full-text searching, using finding aids with a controlled vocabulary (e.g., indexes or tables of contents) can help guide researchers to the content they are seeking with fewer irrelevant results. This chapter identifies leading general legal resources and provides strategies for approaching your research.

II. Major Commercial Databases

There are two major commercial legal research databases, Lexis and Westlaw. Bloomberg Law is also a sizable system, but it is newer and currently lacks some of the content, features, and functionality of the other two. All three systems have a main search bar that will run a full-text search throughout the database. They also have links to collections of materials, grouped by resource type (e.g., cases), jurisdiction, or practice area. Each has its own citator for updating primary sources of law and to assist you in expanding your research.[1] Content in Lexis and Westlaw includes primary and secondary legal resources covering federal law and all fifty states; however, there are some key differences. Most notably: (1) their case coverage is substantially similar, but there isn't identical overlap; (2) each resource has different secondary sources;[2] (3) the editorially selected annotations are not the same; and (4) the systems used to connect cases to each other based on the topics addressed in those cases varies.[3]

Getting into Indiana materials in Lexis and Westlaw is straightforward. From Westlaw's main page, go to the "State Materials" tab and then select Indiana. The process is similar in Lexis, just click on the "State" tab and choose Indiana. In Bloomberg Law, click "All Legal Content" on the homepage. Adjust the chosen organization to "Select Sources by U.S. Jurisdiction." Use the carrot next to "State Law" to expand its options and check the box next to Indiana. Alternatively, if you want to pull up a known resource within

---

1. These are KeyCite in Westlaw, Shepard's in Lexis, and BCite in Bloomberg Law. BCite is a more limited citator than Shepard's or KeyCite. For an in-depth comparison between these tools, see Paul Hellyer, *Evaluating Shepard's, KeyCite, and BCite for Case Validation Accuracy*, 110 Law Libr. J. 449 (2018).

2. For a resource to be included, it must be owned by the database's publisher or licensed from another company. As an example, LexisNexis owns all Matthew Bender publications. Consequently, these resources appear in Lexis, but not in Westlaw.

3. Lexis uses a less robust text-driven topical scheme to provide similar information, while the digest and West Key Number System are exclusive to Westlaw.

any of these databases, begin typing its title into the main search bar. All three systems have an auto-populate feature that will suggest resources as you enter the title, and you can simply select the resource from the generated list. Similarly, if you know the citation to the source you want to access, searching by its citation in the search bar will take you directly to it.

III. Free & Low-Cost Resources

In addition to the principal databases for legal research, there are numerous free and low-cost resources containing cases, laws, and analytical materials. Table 2-1 lists some of these resources. These affordable options are useful alternatives, particularly when you don't have access to Bloomberg Law, Lexis, or Westlaw.

Table 2-1. Free & Low-Cost Resources

Name	Description	Free or Low-Cost	Link
Fastcase	Content includes primary sources of federal and state law.[4] Secondary sources available through recent partnership with HeinOnline, the acquisition of Loislaw, and incorporation of the LexBlog network. Has a citator (i.e., Authority Check) for determining whether a case is still good law.	Low-cost[5]	fc7.fastcase.com

---

4. Includes Indiana Supreme Court cases back to 1885 and Indiana Court of Appeals opinions from 1891 onward.

5. Until recently, there were two leading low-cost legal research platforms, Casemaker and Fastcase. In 2021, the two companies announced their merger, and are now known only as Fastcase. All state bar associations and many local and specialty bar associations offer Fastcase to their members free of charge.

FindLaw	This database provides access to federal and state cases, statutes, and regulations.[6] US Supreme Court cases are available from 1893 onward; lower federal and state court coverage varies.	Free	www.findlaw.com
Google Scholar	Provides Google search capabilities for a large number of state and federal court cases and legal periodicals. Doesn't technically have a citator but includes information about where a case has been cited.	Free	scholar.google.com
Justia	Consists mostly of primary materials linked from federal and state websites.	Free	www.justia.com
LII	Access to federal and state cases, statutes, and regulations, often linking out to state websites for state materials; it also includes access to the US Constitution, foreign and international materials, and uniform laws.	Free	www.law.cornell.edu

A. Government Websites

There is a wealth of legal materials available on government websites. This is perhaps unsurprising because federal, state, and local governments create a significant amount of legal information. While government websites are great for accessing primary sources of law, they commonly have weak search capabilities and a dearth of analytical secondary sources and practical guidance. They are also normally not ideal resources for older materials. For example, IN.gov is the official website of the State of Indiana. The interface is modern and sophisticated, with browsing and search functionality. In its main menu, the "Government" tab leads you to information and resources for Indiana's legislative and judicial branches and prominent entities within the executive branch.

---

6. FindLaw provides access to state statutes and regulations by linking directly to state websites.

IV. Developing a Research Plan

It is a mistake to rush to your computer and begin running searches before developing a research strategy for your legal research problem. Prior to beginning your research, it's beneficial to consider a couple of initial issues, including identifying what legal questions you need to answer and what information you already have. Also, determine the scope of your project by reflecting on the work product requested. Are you researching to draft a memo? A brief or some other form of persuasive writing? Will the tone be analytical? Subjective? After you've completed a little background research, you ought to also consider what criteria should be used to evaluate your results and how you can use what you've already found to locate more and, perhaps, better information. Your answers to these questions will guide your research efforts.

Doing some preliminary planning prior to beginning your research will save you time and yield better results. The steps outlined below are designed to help frame your problem so that your research can be focused and effective.

(1)   First, you should carefully read the problem you must answer or the research task you've been given by your supervising attorney. Review (and re-review) the assignment or case file, and any other information available to you. As you do so, jot down some preliminary notes and any thoughts or impressions you have.

(2)   Next, you need to identify the important legal issues involved. What type of action is it—a tort claim, a criminal case, or something else?

(3)   The unique facts and circumstances of each case impact how the law is applied. Based on your file review and the legal issues you've spotted, reach a preliminary determination of critical facts. For example, if it's a landlord-tenant case, how many months have passed since the tenant paid rent? The facts help you investigate, strategize, and anticipate legal outcomes for your client.

(4)   At this point, make sure that you know which jurisdiction's law will be controlling. Is this a federal or state case? If it's a state case, in which state, county, and district (if applicable) will it be heard? If federal, what circuit is it in?

(5)   Based upon your initial review, generate a list of keywords based on the legal and factual issues and jurisdiction. For example, if it's a

landlord-tenant case, you would include terminology like landlord, tenant, apartment, lease, breach of contract, warranty of habitability, and so forth. The jurisdiction will determine whether you should search for federal or a specific state's law.

(6)   Now you are finally ready to hit the books and search engines! Fight the urge to go directly to the main search box and begin running searches in Lexis and Westlaw's massive databases. You will waste time and your results will be inferior. Instead, obtain an overview from secondary sources or the Internet. Take the time to orient yourself, particularly if you are unfamiliar with the area of law or topic.

(7)   Find and review several good secondary sources on your research topic. Use the footnotes and other references in those sources to find relevant cases, statutes, and regulations. Secondary sources can lead you right to the leading authorities in a particular area of law, saving you time.

(8)   Read and take notes on the primary materials you have found. Remember that the research process is not a strictly linear one. At times, for example, you may have to go back a step or two and find additional secondary sources to improve your understanding, or you may find that you need to tweak your search terms.

(9)   Use citators—BCite in Bloomberg Law, Shepard's in Lexis, or Key-Cite in Westlaw—to expand and update the primary law you've found. These tools can help you verify that a case, statute, or regulation is still "good law" and lead you to related primary and secondary materials.

(10)   Finally, you are ready to put pen to paper. Use the fruits of your research to organize, outline, and draft your memo or other work product.

V. Generating Keywords

Before diving into legal databases or print resources you need to develop a list of terms based on the factual circumstances, legal issues, and desired outcome of your research problem. You will use this list of words to look up terms in an index or table of contents or to search full text in a legal database. There are several different strategies for generating search terms. To help us apply these strategies, let's use a hypothetical scenario. Your client is the landlord of an apartment complex in Terre Haute, Indiana. One of her tenants has failed to pay rent for June, July, and August. Meanwhile, the tenant continues to live in the landlord's building. She has come to you for help collecting the overdue rent and evicting the non-paying tenant. You've been asked to prepare a short, objective legal analysis of the landlord's failure to pay rent and eviction case against the tenant.

One method of identifying keywords is through use of "reporter's questions." Essentially, asking yourself "who, what, when, where, and how" as it relates to your legal problem.

- **Who:** Determine who the parties are that are involved in your research problem. Is it a person? A corporate entity? If you're representing a person, are they a child or do they have some diminished capacity?

- **What:** What legal issue(s) are present that you need to research? What are the material (i.e., legally significant) facts?

- **When:** When did the situation giving rise to the legal problem occur? Timing is very important in legal situations as it determines the law in effect and timeframes for statutes of limitations and similar rules.

- **Where:** This is the point where you select the relevant jurisdiction. Where did the major events take place? Is this a federal or state law issue (or both)?

- **How:** Are there any parameters for your legal research? Which resources are available to you? Has a supervisor recommended that you look in a specific source?

Another way to come up with research terms is using the TARPP technique. TARPP is a mnemonic device to assist you in analyzing the facts of a legal problem. It represents: thing (or subject matter); cause of action; relief sought; persons (or parties); and place. Using our landlord-tenant hypothetical, the TARPP technique could generate keywords like this:

- **Things:** lease, apartment, missed rent payments, back rent

- **Action:** suit to obtain missed rent payments

- **Remedy:** payment of missed rent, any other penalties eligible, termination of lease, and ejection of tenant

- **Persons or Parties:** landlord and tenant

- **Place:** private, residential, apartment building

Regardless of which method you used to generate key terms, try to expand your list by thinking of synonyms for those terms. The language used by the court or in the statute may not exactly match the terminology you initially thought of. It's essential to think in terms of both breadth (e.g., patio—porch—deck) and depth (animal—wild/exotic animal—snake—cobra). As you research, you will likely encounter additional terms, including legal "terms of art" in the practice areas you are researching. Add these to your initial list. Use this list of words to search in a finding aid, such as an index or table of contents, or to search full text.

Another important consideration are the areas of law that may be implicated. This will dictate the type of legal information you need to find. For example, there are likely to be statutes setting forth the responsibilities of both the landlord and the tenant, as well as cases interpreting and applying these statutes.

VI. Search Strategies and Constructing Search Queries

While a quick internet search can give you background information, remember that you are a professional being paid for your expert advice, analysis, and opinion. It is insufficient, and possibly detrimental to your client and your professional reputation, to begin and end your research without finding the controlling cases, statutes, and regulations. Your conclusions need to be rooted in reliable primary sources of law sourced from accurate and up-to-date resources.

Print resources remain a vital part of legal research. To assist researchers, print volumes have a table of contents and, typically, an index. The table of contents is located at the beginning. It outlines the topics contained in the volume in order. Usually, the table of contents will include different levels of headings (e.g., chapter, sections, subsections, etc.). For each level it provides the title and corresponding page numbers. Reading the table of contents is a good way to familiarize yourself with the material covered in the volume and to quickly find content related to your specific research need. Indexes appear at the end of the volume. An index is an alphabetized list of topics with references to the corresponding pages within the text. Like the table of contents, it tells you where information on a particular subject can be found within the volume.

Legal research databases are also fundamental research tools. One of the most straightforward ways to access content in the legal research databases is by citation. If you have a known citation to a case or statute, simply type it into the main search box. Bloomberg Law, Lexis, and Westlaw will recognize the citation and take you directly into the associated document.

Another way to search is by topic. In Lexis, click the Topics tab to see a list of available subject areas. Using our landlord-tenant example, we could select "Real Property Law" and click "Landlord & Tenant." That retrieves all content related to this topic within the database. Similarly, in Westlaw, selecting "Practice areas" from the homepage provides a list of topics linked to subject-specific resources.

There are three principal types of searches that can be run in the legal research databases: *natural language* ("Google-type" searching); *terms and connectors* (also sometimes referred to as *Boolean* searching); and *template* (or *segment*) searching. Pick the right kind of search for your research need. Conventional wisdom is that terms and connectors searching is usually the preferred method if comprehensive results are desired, that is, if your goal is to find all the cases or other sources on a topic. In contrast, natural language searching is ordinarily more appropriate if you are looking for a sample of relevant cases or secondary sources as part of more general or preliminary research.

No matter which type of search you choose, use information about the jurisdiction, source material, or your specific research problem to narrow the content being searched. This will increase the efficiency of your research, by limiting the number of results you must review and saving valuable time. Additionally, it will help control costs associated with your research. For example, if you know you are looking for an Indiana statute, get into the *Indiana Code* prior to running your search.[7]

For terms and connector searches, you must be precise and understand the commands used by that provider. Spaces have different meanings depending on which database you are using. Spaces are treated as an "and" connector in Bloomberg Law and "or" in Westlaw, while Lexis's algorithm interprets the space based on its assessment of the search's terms. The order of search terms also matters. In terms and connectors searches *or* is always processed first; proximity operators are processed next; *and* is processed after that; and *and not* or *but not* are processed last. For example, if you search Indiana state cases in Lexis and Westlaw using the following terms and connectors search: "landlord and tenant /s habit!" you will retrieve remarkably different results.[8] Finally, follow the K.I.S.S.[9] principle when crafting search queries. Overcomplicated search strings can leave you with limited (or zero) relevant results.

Tables 2-2 through 2-4 provide commonly used connectors, proximity commands, and expanders and wildcards available in the three databases.

---

7. Common ways to pre-filter or narrow the content prior to running a search are by jurisdiction, type (or category) of material, and practice area or topic.

8. Westlaw returns 37 cases versus Lexis's 39. Moreover, using the default sort of relevance, the first 3 cases in each set of results are completely different.

9. K.I.S.S. stands for "keep it simple and straightforward."

Notice that the signals telling the database how to process search terms differs. Be sure to use the appropriate signals for the system you are using.

Table 2-2. Connectors

Description	Bloomberg Law	Lexis	Westlaw	Sample Search
both terms present	and	and	and &	lease and agreement
either term present	or	or	space or	liable or responsible (in all 3); liable responsible (in Westlaw)
exclude a term	not and not but not	and not	% but not	collateral and not estoppel (in Bloomberg or Lexis); collateral % estoppel (in Westlaw)

Table 2-3. Proximity (within sentence, paragraph, or number of words)

Description	Bloomberg Law	Lexis	Westlaw	Sample Search
terms must appear in the same sentence	s/ /s /sent	/s w/s w/sent (database equivalent of near/25)	/s w/s	custody /s guidelines
terms must appear in the same paragraph	p/ /p /para	/p w/p w/para (database equivalent of near/75)	/p w/p	patent /p application
terms must be within n words	/# w/# n/#	/# w/# near/#	/#	breach /5 duty

Table 2-4. Expanders & Wildcards

Description	Bloomberg Law	Lexis	Westlaw	Sample Search
expand root term by any # of letters	!	!	!	employ! (finds employ, employment, employer, etc.)
variations for single character in term	*	*	*	wom*n (finds woman or women)
plurals	check "include word variations" on search screen	automati-cally searches regular plurals	automati-cally searches plurals and possessives	misdemeanor (finds misdemeanors too in Westlaw and Lexis)
hyphenate	include all possible variations separated by or	include all possible variations separated by or	hyphenated form automati-cally retrieves all variations of compound words	at-will (searches for atwill, at will, or at-will in Westlaw); type out at-will or "at will" in Bloom-berg Law and Lexis

Many legal documents share a common structure. For instance, cases typically contain the same components. These include the name of the case, the date of the opinion, the judge(s) authoring the opinion, etc. Conducting a template or segment search allows you to limit your search results to a specific segment. For example, if you wanted to find opinions written by Indiana Supreme Court Chief Justice Loretta H. Rush, a segment search would be invaluable. To access a template for segment searching in Westlaw or Lexis, navigate to the content you wish to search (e.g., Cases > Indiana > Indiana Supreme Court). Click on the advanced search option to pull up the template. Then, enter "Loretta Rush" into the relevant segment (e.g., Written By (WB)). Once you run the search, the database will retrieve all opinions written by Chief Justice Rush.

VII. Processing and Evaluating Search Results

After running a search, you will need to sift through and evaluate your results. Frequently, you will retrieve far too many results to examine them all. Westlaw and Lexis have built-in features designed to assist you with this conundrum by helping you quickly narrow your results. In both databases, results can be post-search filtered by a number of different elements, including document type (i.e., cases, statutes, etc.), jurisdiction, specific court, date, and by "search within" for a particular word or phrase.

If your initial searches fail to return the information you are seeking, don't hesitate to edit your search terms and strings and re-run a search. Lexis retains your search history for ninety days and Westlaw maintains it for a year, so you can look back on prior searches and results for quite a long time.

VIII. Organizing Your Research

Organize and keep track of the sources you find by utilizing the notetaking, highlighting, and folder features to annotate and save relevant cases and materials. Research is often a time-consuming and byzantine process. Organizing your research can help you stay focused and efficient. The major legal databases allow you to store selected content in folders for easy retrieval. Use these folders to save the resources you've found. While reading, use the highlighting and notetaking capabilities to capture relevant passages for further review. Above all, take time to experiment with the database tools and to develop your own organization process. For more ideas about how to organize your research, see Chapter 10, Research Strategies.

Chapter 3

Secondary Sources

In law, secondary sources explain, interpret, or analyze the law, but are not the "law" itself. In contrast, primary legal materials are the laws and rules issued by governing bodies. In the US system, these are cases, statutes, regulations, constitutions, executive orders, and proclamations. Generally speaking, any legal materials that are not primary materials are considered secondary. Secondary sources are never binding or controlling of the outcome in a legal case or dispute; however, used effectively, they can persuade a court (or another adjudicator) to reach one conclusion over another. The level of persuasiveness of secondary sources varies depending upon several factors, including the type of secondary source and its author. Secondary sources can help you understand and apply legal principles, assist you in the development of keywords, and contain useful references to related primary materials.

Use secondary sources at several different stages of your research process. At the beginning, secondary sources can help you generate search terms, develop an understanding of the legal concepts involved, and lead you to related primary authority. The type of secondary source you'll want to consult will change as you move through the research process. For example, at the start of your research, legal encyclopedias and practitioner-focused secondary sources are excellent ways to get a quick overview of an unfamiliar area of law. As your understanding grows and the focus of your research narrows, you'll want to consult more detailed secondary sources such as treatises or the *American Law Reports*. Returning to secondary sources as your research progresses is helpful as well. Secondary sources can help you organize and develop complex arguments, locate additional primary authority to bolster your analysis, and verify your understanding of the leading cases, statutes, or other primary sources on a topic.

There are eight commonly used types of law-related secondary sources: legal encyclopedias, *American Law Reports* (ALR); practice aids, formbooks, and CLE publications; law review articles and other periodicals; treatises and monographs; looseleaf services; Restatements; uniform laws; and jury instructions. This section explores each type of secondary source and provides techniques for effective and efficient secondary source research.

I. Tips for Researching Secondary Sources

- **Generate a list of keywords and phrases.** Before diving into a secondary source, develop a list of keywords based on facts and legal concepts relevant to your research. To further develop ideas about which keywords and phrases to employ while using a secondary source, try running preliminary full-text searches and scanning the index and table of contents.

- **Crowdsource.** Obtain recommendations for which resources to consult from colleagues with knowledge of the subject area.

- **Use available finding aids.** Most secondary sources, whether in print or electronic format, have finding aids such as tables of contents or indexes to assist researchers in identifying relevant topics within the resource.

- **Try multiple full-text searches.** If researching electronically, run different natural language or terms and connectors searches in the publication using various combinations of your keywords. Chapter 2 addressed how to construct terms and connectors searches for different commercial databases.

- **Identify sections relevant to your issue.** Then, carefully read the text to assist in your comprehension of the state of the law in your area of research.

- **Use cited references.** Look at the references, including footnotes, to identify primary authority that you may want to consult. Find and read any primary authority referred to by the secondary source.

- **Update the publication.** Use the *scope note* to update online research and the appropriate editions, *supplement*, or *pocket parts* in print.[1]

---

1. A scope note is often indicated by a lower-case "i," standing for information, and typically provides a broad description of the source, its author or editor, when

II. Legal Encyclopedias

Similar to traditional encyclopedias, legal encyclopedias are alphabetically arranged collections of short articles on a wide variety of topics. Encyclopedia entries tend to be brief as their objective is to summarize the law on a given topic. The articles may identify areas of conflict between jurisdictions but do not provide in-depth analysis. Legal encyclopedias emphasize breadth of topic coverage over depth of analysis and are useful for gaining background information and generating keywords. They also contain references to primary sources of law in their footnotes.

There are two kinds of legal encyclopedias: national and state. *American Jurisprudence, Second Edition* (Am. Jur. 2d) and *Corpus Juris Secundum* (CJS) are the two national-level encyclopedias. Am. Jur. 2d and CJS cover multiple jurisdictions. Both national and state encyclopedias contain numerous footnotes. National encyclopedia footnotes reference cases from jurisdictions nationwide. In contrast, footnotes in state encyclopedias cite authorities only from within that jurisdiction. Footnotes in the national encyclopedias are often older; however, you can use a citator (e.g., Shepard's or KeyCite) to identify more recent authority. The national encyclopedias also cross-reference the West Key Number System, *American Law Reports*, and other resources.

A. National Encyclopedias

Am. Jur. 2d and CJS are collections of articles covering all areas of American law, both substantive and procedural, as well as federal and state jurisdictions. Each article examines and summarizes broad principles of a legal concept and provides references to supporting primary materials as well as additional secondary sources. National encyclopedias can be particularly helpful for finding out how federal courts or courts in other state jurisdictions have examined and treated the issue you are researching. For example, if the state of the law related to your problem is ambiguous in Indiana, you may want to identify court decisions with similar fact patterns from other jurisdictions to support your position. Am. Jur. 2d and CJS are held by most law libraries in print. Online, Am. Jur. 2d is accessible on both Lexis and Westlaw while CJS is available on Westlaw, but not included on Lexis.

---

appropriate, and the frequency with which it is updated. In print, updates to a secondary source may come in the form of a supplement, a slim paper-back volume either following an individual hard-back volume, or following the entire set of the print source; alternatively, updates may come in the form of a pocket part, a slim paper volume that fits in the inside back cover of the hard-bound volume.

B. State Encyclopedias

Many states also have their own state-level legal encyclopedia. For issues controlled by state law, it is preferable to begin your research in a state-specific legal encyclopedia rather than Am. Jur. 2d or CJS. The entries in each state's encyclopedia are particular to the law in that jurisdiction and contain supporting references to that state's cases. Indiana's legal encyclopedia is *West's Indiana Law Encyclopedia* and—because Thomson West is its sole publisher—it is available only on Westlaw or in print. This is a thirty-volume set. All of the articles in the encyclopedia are based on Indiana statutes and rules, case opinions, law reviews, state attorney general's opinions, U.S. Supreme Court cases, and other federal cases originating within the jurisdiction. It contains discussions of legal principles, including any applicable exceptions or limitations, as well as guidance on how to handle certain situations. The supporting footnotes reference major Indiana cases on the subject and other primary authority.

C. Using Encyclopedias

When using a legal encyclopedia online you have the option of running a full-text search (either using natural language or terms and connectors) or using a finding aid, like the table of contents. To navigate to legal encyclopedias on Westlaw, click on the "Secondary Sources" link on the homepage. Under "By Type," you can find legal encyclopedias by clicking the "Jurisprudence and Encyclopedias" link. Here you will find all of Westlaw's legal encyclopedias arranged in alphabetical order. You can use the filters on the left to refine the list by publication series, topic (i.e., practice area), jurisdiction, or titles that you had previously designated as favorites. To pull up the *Indiana Law Encyclopedia* you can either scroll through the alphabetical list or filter by jurisdiction and select Indiana. Click on the hyperlink to *Indiana Law Encyclopedia* to navigate to a page with the encyclopedia's table of contents and search bar at the top. Anything you search in the search bar will only be run through this particular publication. When using the table of contents, click on the + next to a topic to expand and view its subtopics until you find the section(s) relevant to your research. Remember that, because the *Indiana Law Encyclopedia* is a Thomson West publication, it is available only on Westlaw and cannot be accessed online through Lexis or any of the other legal databases.

While the core volumes of Am. Jur. 2d can be found on Lexis and Westlaw, only Westlaw includes supplemental resources within the Am. Jur. publication family, such as *American Jurisprudence Legal Forms 2d*, *American Jurisprudence Proof of Facts*, and *American Jurisprudence Trials*. In Lexis, locate the national encyclopedias by clicking on "Secondary Materials," then selecting "Treatises, Practice Guides & Jurisprudence." In Lexis and Westlaw, you can also access content by beginning to type the title of the source into the main search box. Both systems have an auto-population feature that will suggest sources within the database.

When using a print legal encyclopedia, always begin by using its index. An index is an alphabetical list of names and subjects typically found at the end of the volume or series. To use an index effectively, search it for one of your core research terms. For best results, use a broad topic. For example, if you wanted to research issues arising out of a case where a child was bitten by a dog, you'd first look for a general term, such as "dogs." Once you've located "Dogs" in the index, you can quickly skim its subtopics to find "Injury to persons by dog." Since you want to get an overview of the potential issues in a dog bite situation, you'd likely gravitate towards "generally, ANIMALS § 67 to 74." This index entry tells you that this information is contained within the Animals volume in sections 67 through 74. Now, all you need to do is find the corresponding volumes by reading the topics printed on the spines of the volumes and flipping to the relevant sections. When you have found the sections, scan the topical outline to get a sense of the subordinate subjects covered under that topic.

III. *American Law Reports*

The *American Law Reports* (ALR) is a multi-volume, multi-series publication that provides an in-depth analysis of very narrow issues of law. Each entry in the ALR is referred to as an article. The ALR is a popular secondary source among legal researchers for two reasons: First, each article provides a state-by-state analysis of the legal question posed, making it a great resource for cross-state comparative research. Second, ALR articles provide a wealth of citations to other primary and secondary sources (particularly cases) to further your research.

In print, the ALR consists of seven series covering all jurisdictions, plus three federal-focused series. Earlier ALR series began each annotation, now called articles, with an illustrative case, followed by the descriptive annotation. More recent series have dropped the illustrative case feature, but the structure of the articles remains the same. Each article consists of the features listed in Table 3-1.

Table 3-1. Features of an ALR Article

Feature	Description
Article Outline	Lengthy table of contents to the article, broken down into discrete topics
Index	Keyword index to the various sections of the article
Table of Cases, Laws, and Rules	Table of authorities for the article—listing all primary sources cited in the article, arranged hierarchically by jurisdiction
Research References	Listing of additional secondary sources to further your research on the topic—this typically refers the reader to other ALR articles, encyclopedia entries, and practice aids.

Two additional features of the ALR are the ALR Index and the ALR Digest. Each ALR series stands alone; therefore the comprehensive Index facilitates finding relevant articles across the series. The ALR Digest provides brief descriptions of each ALR article, as another means of selecting relevant content to research.

In addition to print, the ALR can also be found online through Lexis or Westlaw. Lexis includes ALR (Second through Seventh) and ALR Federal (First through Third). Westlaw has the complete ALR series, including ALR (First through Seventh), ALR Federal (First through Third), the ALR Index, and the ALR Digest. The *American Law Reports* is found under Secondary Sources (Westlaw) or Secondary Materials (Lexis).

There are a few advantages of using the ALR online. First, most cited references are hyperlinked, facilitating the transition to reading a cited case, statute, or secondary source. Second, articles are continuously updated, to add additional relevant cases and references. Westlaw recently introduced another helpful feature to its ALR annotations, "Locate Authority by Jurisdiction." This menu on the left-hand side of the screen allows you to select one or more jurisdictions to focus on in the article; when selected, any citations to those jurisdictions are highlighted, making it much easier to see where your jurisdictions appear in the text of the annotation. ALR articles are typically very lengthy, printing out at 100+ pages, so this jurisdiction locator feature can be an efficient way to navigate through the annotation.

Although the length of an ALR article can seem unwieldy, the citations it provides are unparalleled by any other secondary source. While you may not find an ALR article on every legal topic, it is well worth your time to see if a relevant ALR article exists for your legal question. If so, the references in the article offer a virtual library of sources to further your research.

IV. Practice Aids, Formbooks, and CLE Publications

Attorneys work in different areas of law and perform many diverse tasks. Practice aids are a broad category of secondary sources that assist lawyers by providing information about the current state of the law in a particular area, give guidance on the best ways to approach specific issues, and supply tools and examples to assist them with completing routine legal matters (e.g., drafting a will). Asking colleagues with experience in the area of law you are researching for their practice aid recommendations is always a good idea. Practice aids are available in print and in commercial databases. To locate a practice aid in Lexis or Westlaw, start in "Secondary Sources/Materials." In Lexis, practice aids are grouped into "Treatises & Practice Guides." In Westlaw, select "Texts & Treatises" and use the filters to refine by "Publication Series" and/or "Jurisdiction." Identify the practice aids by looking for the words "deskbook," "handbook," "manual," or "practice" in the title.

In addition to the major commercial databases, Thomson Reuters' Practical Law database includes standard documents and clauses, as well as annotated checklists. Materials can be filtered by practice area, jurisdiction, resource type, or a combination of all three categories. To access Indiana-focused practitioner materials, click the "Jurisdictions" tab and select Indiana. You can then use the filters on the left to narrow by type of resource (e.g., standard documents) and/or practice area (e.g., labor and employment). Lexis offers a similar product called Lexis Practice Advisor®. It includes practice notes, forms, and checklists in a variety of complex practice areas.

Document drafting is a common task in many areas of legal practice. Attorneys frequently use formbooks to help identify essential language for specific types of legal documents. Formbooks assist in making this task easier by providing sample documents and lists of recommended elements to include. Transactional practice areas, like taxation, often require the use of specific forms which are also included in formbooks. To find Indiana legal forms in print, access a library's catalog, run a subject search by "Forms (Law)—Indiana" or keyword search for a combination of the terms "form," "law," and "Indiana." Be mindful that every legal situation is unique and has different requirements. When using a formbook, it is critical to exercise your own judgment and tailor your work product to meet the needs of your specific situation.

Bloomberg Law, Lexis, and Westlaw all contain legal forms from a variety of practice areas. Bloomberg Law has the Transactional Intelligence Center which includes sample agreements and clauses, its Draft Analyzer tool,[2] and drafting guidance. In Lexis you can access forms a few ways. One method is to select "Forms" under "Content Type" and then narrow by jurisdiction or practice area. This takes you to a template where you can do a segment search for relevant forms. Another way is to navigate to "Secondary Materials" and look for resources which include forms, such as *Indiana Pleading and Practice with Forms*. If you're unsure whether a particular resource contains forms and it isn't clear from its title, click on its scope note and read the description which will usually indicate if the book includes forms. Access forms in Westlaw by clicking "Forms" on its homepage. This takes you to the database's Form Finder where you can run a search in the main search box for forms or browse forms by state or topic.

Completion of annual Continuing Legal Education (CLE) courses is required by most state bar associations. Attorneys must attend a minimum number of class hours to maintain an active license to practice law. CLE courses cover the entire spectrum of topics related to the practice of law, including ethics and professional responsibility. Generally, CLE speakers are attorneys and judges with expertise in the area of law covered by the program. In addition to their presentations, these speakers often provide supplemental materials for attendees. Typically, CLE resources include sample forms and documents, as well as detailed explanations of techniques, strategies, and practical guidance. Organizations like the Indiana Continuing Legal Education Forum (ICLEF[3]), which offer CLE courses, also produce

---

2. Draft Analyzer allows users to "drag and drop" draft contract language into the system and compare it with existing language pulled from agreements and organizational documents filed on EDGAR.

3. Visit the website at https://www.iclef.org/.

accompanying publications helpful for handling a range of legal matters. Westlaw offers CLE content in its "CLE and Seminar Materials" section (in Secondary Sources). Be cautious about the currency of CLE materials. While older CLE content can still be helpful, look first for courses given within the past few years. Because CLE materials aren't updated in a regular and uniform way, older resources may contain information that is outdated and no longer useful. Table 3-2 lists Indiana Practice Aids and Formbooks and where to find them.

Table 3-2. Indiana Practice Aids and Formbooks

Title	Type of Resource	Where Found
Indiana Practice Series	General	Westlaw, print
Practical Law Indiana	General	Westlaw
Practice Advisor Indiana	General	Lexis
Coalition for Court Access	Focused on areas of law frequently encountered by self-represented litigants (e.g., small claims, family court, traffic, etc.)	Open access: https://indianaleg-alhelp.org/court-forms/
Appellate Handbook for Indiana Lawyers	Litigation: Appellate	Lexis, print
Indiana Evidence Courtroom Manual	Litigation: Civil and Criminal	Lexis, print
Indiana Pleading and Practice with Forms	Litigation: Civil and Criminal	Lexis, print
Indiana Search and Seizure Courtroom Manual	Litigation: Criminal	Lexis, print
Indiana Model/Pattern Jury Instructions	Litigation: Civil and Criminal	Lexis, Westlaw, print
Indiana Trial Evidence Manual	Litigation: Civil and Criminal	Lexis, print
Midwest Transaction Guide	Transactional	Lexis, print

CCH Indiana State Tax Reporter	Transactional: State Tax	Lexis, VitalLaw,[4] print
Henry's Indiana Probate Law and Practice	Transactional: Trusts & Estates	Lexis, print
Indiana Estate Planning and Probate Practice (includes forms)	Transactional: Trusts & Estates	Lexis, print

V. Legal Periodicals

Legal periodicals cover a broad spectrum of publications, essentially any legal secondary source that is published periodically. Practically, periodicals are divided into two sub-categories: Bar Journals and Law Reviews.

A. Bar Journals

A bar journal refers to the publication of a bar association. The content of a bar journal is typically written by practitioners and judges, and focused on practice tips and legal news in that jurisdiction. Most, if not all, state bar associations have a bar journal. The bar journal for the Indiana State Bar Association is *Res Gestae*. Published in a magazine format, this monthly publication contains snippets on recent Indiana cases and legislative developments, articles on legal news in Indiana, trends in law practice, and practical advice. It also contains membership news and advertisements for attorney job openings across the state. Members of the Indiana State Bar Association receive a complimentary print subscription to *Res Gestae*, as well as digital access to the publication from the bar association website. Several subscription databases, including Lexis, Westlaw, and HeinOnline, also contain *Res Gestae*, but coverage varies, as depicted in Table 3-3.

---

4. VitalLaw is another commercial legal database, owned by Wolters Kluwer. It is discussed further in Chapter 8.

Table 3-3. *Res Gestae* on Westlaw, Lexis, and HeinOnline

	Westlaw	Lexis	HeinOnline
Res Gestae	Full coverage 1994 to present; select coverage 1985 to 1994	Full coverage 2007 to present	Full coverage from inception, 1957 to present

B. Law Reviews

Law reviews refer to the academic law journals typically published by law schools. Law review articles are written by legal scholars; these articles tend to be much longer, fifty or more pages, and are heavily footnoted. The content of a law review article tends to be unique, as compared to other secondary sources. In a law review article, a scholar often tackles a divisive topic, a hotly debated legal issue, a circuit split, or a new development in law. Even for existing legal issues, the author will offer a new argument or approach to the legal problem. For these reasons, law reviews can be an excellent source when your research into other secondary sources fails to bear fruit.

Most, if not all, law schools publish law reviews. Some are subject-specific, like the *Indiana Journal of Global Legal Studies*,[5] while others are more open. You may find some law reviews that are jurisdiction-specific, but that is rare. The *Indiana Law Review*,[6] for instance, published by Indiana University's Robert H. McKinney School of Law in Indianapolis, Indiana, has one issue a year dedicated to developments in Indiana law, but the other three issues are more general. Likewise, the *Indiana Law Journal*,[7] published by Indiana University Maurer School of Law, in Bloomington, Indiana, is a general-focus journal, with no issues focused on Indiana specifically. When you are looking for law review articles in furtherance of your research, therefore, it is not advisable to narrow by jurisdiction, as that will severely limit your results and may exclude relevant content.

Legal periodicals are included in a number of commercial databases. Lexis and Westlaw each have a Law Reviews & Journals category within their secondary source collections. For both databases, coverage varies by title. One helpful feature of law journal research on Lexis and Westlaw is the ability to

---

5. The website is https://www.repository.law.indiana.edu/ijgls/.
6. The website is https://mckinneylaw.iu.edu/ilr/index.html.
7. The website is https://www.repository.law.indiana.edu/ilj/.

seek out journals by topic. If you were researching a patent law issue, for example, you could easily find all the intellectual property-focused law reviews on Lexis or Westlaw. Both platforms also offer the advantage of access to a citator. When you access a law review article on Lexis or Westlaw, you will be able to see all cases and secondary sources that have cited that article, facilitating your search for related materials. HeinOnline has a far broader collection of law journals in its Law Journal Library. Hein collects more titles and digitizes the full run of all journals in its collection.[8] Hein also includes more foreign and international law journals, as well as a large collection of bar journals, making it an excellent resource when conducting research in legal periodicals.

Finally, while most categories of secondary sources, such as treatises and encyclopedias, are only available in print or through a subscription service, legal periodicals, and in particular, academic law reviews, are a notable exception. Not only are they available in print and through subscription services, many are increasingly available for free online. When conducting research in law journals, there are several free sites you may want to consult. First, the journal's website. Many journals will put their most recent issue, and often a short archive of previous issues, on their website for free. Even journals that do not provide free access to their most recent issue will typically at a minimum provide the table of contents to their latest issue. Second, law school libraries have begun creating digital repositories to preserve their school's publications, including law journals, in a free, online format. Often these libraries will offer free digital access to the back issues of their law school's journals. The digital repository from Indiana University Maurer School of Law's Jerome Hall Law Library, for instance, offers the full run of all Maurer's law journals.[9] Finally, another source to be aware of when seeking out relevant law journal content is the Social Science Research Network (SSRN).[10] This free online source has a growing collection of legal content, and is particularly helpful for finding *pre-prints*, versions of articles awaiting publication. If you are researching a relatively new issue in law, pre-published articles may be a critical source for your research. You can run a broad search

---

8. Select journals include a short embargo period on their most recent issues.

9. The website is https://www.repository.law.indiana.edu/journals/. One Maurer journal, the *Indiana Journal of Global Legal Studies*, has a one-year embargo for articles authored by Maurer faculty and students and a five-year embargo for all other articles. For all other journals, the digital repository offers access to the entire run.

10. The website is https://www.ssrn.com.

across the entire SSRN platform, or select the browse option to filter down to "Social Sciences," then the "Legal Scholarship Network."

VI. Treatises and Other Books

Treatises are in-depth analyses of a single area of law and can be substantive or procedural. They are typically written by professors, legal scholars, or high-profile jurists. If sufficiently preeminent, treatises may be cited to in case opinions or court documents. The classic example is *Wright and Miller's Federal Practice and Procedure*, the leading authority on federal practice. According to Thomson West, it has been cited in case opinions over 90,000 times. Like other secondary sources, treatises also have citations to related primary authority and other secondary sources. Consequently, they are a great tool to quickly zero in on the major cases on a particular point of law. Study aids and hornbooks are a subset of treatises designed to assist law students in preparing for class and studying for exams.

Treatises are usually owned by a single publisher. Keep this in mind as you research and understand that you will not be able to access the same treatise in all of the legal databases. As an example, *Wright and Miller* is available only on Westlaw because it is a Thomson West publication. In Lexis, the major federal procedural treatise is *Moore's Federal Practice* (which is likewise unavailable on Westlaw). In print, treatises and monographs are updated by the publication of a new edition, insertion of loose-leaf pages, or the addition of a pocket part at the end of the volume. Electronically, you can determine how current a treatise is by consulting its scope note.

If you aren't sure which treatises to look at when researching, consider using a treatise finder.[11] Georgetown's Law Library has a series of treatise finders organized by practice area. For each treatise in the finder, it provides the title, author(s), and a brief description of the work. Icons are used to indicate which works are considered preeminent on that topic, to designate the legal database containing the treatise (*e.g.*, Westlaw or Lexis) if available electronically, and to specify whether the title is helpful as a study aid for law students. Library catalogs are another excellent resource for finding treatises and books on a particular area of law. Run a subject search for your topic within the library's catalog to determine its call number range. Once you've

---

11. The website is https://guides.ll.georgetown.edu/home/treatise-finders.

found the physical location of that call number, scan the titles in and around that area to find books germane to your research.

VII. Looseleaf Services

Looseleaf services are compilations of primary and secondary materials in a particular practice area. They're called *looseleafs* because, in print, they are published in binders with removable and replaceable individual pages (leaves). This format is used to enable the publication to be updated easily. This is crucial as looseleafs are a current awareness tool used by lawyers to keep abreast of the current state of the law. Practice areas covered by looseleaf services tend to be heavily regulated and complex (e.g., federal and state taxation, immigration, and employment law). Looseleafs reprint and collocate related statutes, regulations, agency decisions, and other guidance documents. They also contain editorial commentary, including analysis, examples, and advice for practitioners. Publication schedules can be daily, weekly, or monthly. Many print looseleafs are now available online. Bloomberg Law[12] and VitalLaw[13] have the largest collections of online looseleaf services. Westlaw also has a couple, mostly in the area of labor and employment law.

VIII. Restatements & Principles of the Law

Restatements of the Law are a series of publications drafted by the American Law Institute (ALI). The intent behind the *Restatements* is to "restate" the common law of a particular legal topic. Members of the ALI take a particular legal issue and draft a rule of law to address the issue, based on how the majority of states have ruled on this issue in their courts. Volumes of the *Restatements* contain these rules of law, followed by comments that explain how the rule was developed. In print, *Restatements* are accompanied by appendix volumes that contain summaries of illustrative cases where this rule has been applied. If your jurisdiction has not ruled on a particular legal issue yet (i.e., it is a *case of first impression*), looking to the black letter language of the *Restatement* can be a strong persuasive argument; in fact, judges will often look to the *Restatements* when rendering a decision in a new area of law.

---

12. Known for its treatises published by Bloomberg BNA.

13. VitalLaw is a database owned by Wolters Kluwer. It contains looseleafs published by the Commerce Clearinghouse (CCH). VitalLaw was previously named Cheetah, and before that, CCH IntelliConnect.

There are *Restatements* in several areas of law, from larger subjects, such as torts, property, and contracts, to more discrete subjects, such as conflict of laws and foreign relations law. In addition to finding these materials in print, researchers can access the *Restatements* through subscriptions to Lexis, Westlaw, or HeinOnline.[14] In Lexis and Westlaw, the *Restatements* are found in the "Secondary Sources/Materials" collections. In HeinOnline, the *Restatements* are located in the "American Law Institute Library." There have been revisions to several of the *Restatements* over the years, with most *Restatements* into their second or third series. The ALI continues to work on revisions and updates to the *Restatements*. You can see a list of their current projects on the ALI website.[15] HeinOnline's "American Law Institute Library" contains the most recent drafts of *Restatement* revisions-in-progress.

Related to the *Restatements* are the ALI's *Principles of Law*. Where the *Restatements* focus on common law and the courts, the *Principles of Law* are intended for other bodies of government, such as legislatures and agencies, and even private parties. Similar to the *Restatements*, the *Principles* offer black-letter law based on the majority of states' treatment of a particular area of law, and include comments, illustrations, and recommendations. *Principles of the Law* cover a broad range of topics, from data privacy to policing to corporate governance. *Principles of the Law* are available in HeinOnline's "American Law Institute Library" and in print.

IX. Uniform Laws

Uniform laws can be thought of similarly to the *Restatements*. While the *Restatements* focus on black-letter common law, uniform laws seek to create black-letter statutory law. Composed by the Uniform Law Commission (ULC), a non-partisan body of lawyers appointed by their state governments to serve in this organization, uniform laws offer suggested statutory text that state legislatures may choose to adopt in whole, in part, or not at all.

The uniform laws are published in print in a series called *Uniform Laws Annotated*. This publication provides the language of each uniform law, highlights state variations, and offers annotations to cases that have applied the law in adopting jurisdictions. *Uniform Laws Annotated* is available online

---

14. Bloomberg Law also has a select collection of Restatements, comprising ten of the twenty areas of law currently covered.

15. American Law Institute, Current Projects, https://www.ali.org/projects/.

through Westlaw. In Westlaw, you also have the advantage of procuring citator information, such as citing references, to see what cases and secondary sources have cited a particular uniform law. The "Refs & Annos" link at the top of a particular uniform law will take you to a page that provides a table of adopting jurisdictions, and where the uniform law is codified in each jurisdiction's code, as well as extensive history notes on that particular uniform law. Lexis also provides access to uniform laws, in a collection called "Uniform Law Commission Acts." This collection provides the draft language of the uniform laws, but does not include citator information or details on adopting jurisdictions. The Uniform Commercial Code, one of the best known and widely adopted uniform laws, is provided separate from this collection in Lexis, but is included in *Uniform Laws Annotated*, in print and on Westlaw. Both Lexis and Westlaw provide access to the uniform laws from their "Statutes" collections.

HeinOnline also includes current and historical versions of the uniform laws, in its "Uniform Law Commission: National Conference of Commissioners on Uniform State Laws" library. In addition to current and archived versions of the uniform laws themselves, Hein's collection includes reference items, such as the proceedings from the annual conference meeting of the Uniform Law Commission, as well as the Commission's handbook.

Finally, if you do not have access to the print or subscription services, the Uniform Law Commission provides complimentary access to the most recent version of each uniform law on its website.[16] Once you select a particular act, the site offers several helpful features. For example, if you pull up the Anatomical Gift Act,[17] the home page provides an interactive enactment map, highlighting which states have enacted the act or are considering it, and tabs above the map provide a list of bill numbers, including the bill's enactment status and sponsor; a summary of the act; and a table of enactment history. Blue tabs at the top of the page provide an "enactment kit," with tools to advocate for your state's adoption of the act; final act documents, including the most recent version of the act, with commentary; bill tracking, for any states with pending legislation; and a committee archive that contains other supporting documentation from the ULC pertaining to the history of the act.

---

16. Uniform Law Commission, Current Acts, https://www.uniformlaws.org/acts/catalog/current.

17. Uniform Law Commission, Anatomical Gift Act, https://www.uniformlaws.org/committees/community-home?CommunityKey=015e18ad-4806-4dff-b011-8e1ebc0d1d0f.

X. Jury Instructions

Jury instructions are a set of guidelines for how a jury should proceed in their deliberations. They include not only instructions on the process juries should follow, but also on the rule of law they should apply when rendering their decision. In jury trials, attorneys may submit their own recommended jury instructions for the judge's consideration, but several entities publish model jury instructions for different legal scenarios as well. Both Lexis and Westlaw have large Jury Instructions collections, including both general model jury instructions, as well as jurisdiction-specific instructions for the majority of states. For Indiana, both databases provide access to *Indiana Model Civil Jury Instructions* and *Indiana Pattern Criminal Jury Instructions*, written by the Indiana Judges Association. Many courts offer their own model jury instructions, often available for free from their website.[18] Model jury instructions serve as a guide for attorneys, moldable to their own clients' cases.

---

18. For example, the Seventh Circuit Court of Appeals offers pattern jury instructions for civil and criminal trials at https://www.ca7.uscourts.gov/pattern-jury-instructions/pattern-jury.htm.

Chapter 4

Constitutions, Statutes, and Court Rules

Constitutions, statutes, and court rules are primary sources of law in our legal system. Consequently, it is essential to develop a familiarity with where to find their text as well as the commonly used secondary sources and other tools that help interpret and apply them. This chapter discusses resources and strategies for effectively and efficiently researching constitutions, statutes, and court rules.

I. Constitutions

Constitutions are broadly written statements setting forth fundamental rights and delegating powers to make rules and laws effectuating those rights to subordinate branches of government. The scope of these rights and powers is almost always defined by case opinions interpreting the provisions. The United States Supreme Court is the ultimate authority on federal constitutional interpretation. Similarly, the Indiana Supreme Court determines the scope of constitutional rights under that state's constitution. While a state's constitution is its highest form of law, the text of a constitutional provision alone is unlikely to fully answer any of your research questions.

Numerous resources containing the text of the federal and state constitutions exist. It is advantageous to look at the constitution in an annotated code so that you not only get the text itself, but also cases and interpretive secondary sources. For example, assume you represent a client sentenced to death for his murder conviction. On appeal, you want to argue that the State of Indiana imposed an unconstitutional religious test when it asked the jurors if they had any religious or moral beliefs which would prevent them from voting for the death penalty. You would like to allege that this violated Article 1, Section 5 of the Constitution of the State of Indiana, stating that "No religious test shall be required as a qualification for any office of trust or profit."

Clearly, the constitutional text is vague and does not directly answer your research question. What constitutes an office of trust or profit? Does it include members of an impaneled jury? Accordingly, you would need to find and review case opinions interpreting and applying the section to similar situations.

A. Locating and Researching the Indiana Constitution

Each state has its own written constitution. These tend to be longer and more detailed than the federal constitution. Since becoming a state in 1816, Indiana has had two constitutions. The Constitution of 1816 was its first and was highly controversial from nearly the beginning. As a result, it was later replaced by the Constitution of 1851, which is still in force. Indiana's amendment procedures are more restrictive than most other jurisdictions because the General Assembly must refer constitutional amendments to amend the constitution, which requires the proposed amendment to be approved in two successive sessions of the Indiana General Assembly before the citizens have the ability to vote on it. Voter approval is required to enact a constitutional amendment in Indiana.

Like the federal constitution, Indiana's constitution is published in the official and unofficial versions of its state code. Many of the commonly encountered state constitutional legal issues involve individual rights. The process for researching the Indiana constitution mirrors that of researching statutes as discussed in section II, below. You would first search for a relevant provision either online or in print. But simply finding a constitutional provision won't answer your research question.

To illustrate, let's return to our earlier example: whether asking jurors if they have any religious or moral beliefs that would prevent them from voting for the death penalty violates Article 1, Section 5 of the Constitution of the State of Indiana. To find the answer, you'd need to perform additional research beyond the text itself. A great place to begin researching this issue is *Burns Indiana Constitution Annotated*. To access *Burns* online, you must use Lexis. Begin typing "Indiana Constitution" into the main search box and select *Burns Indiana Constitution Annotated* when the option auto populates. When the Constitution of the State of Indiana 1851 appears, you can either expand the table of contents and browse to Article 1, Section 5 or run a full-text search (e.g., religious /2 test). Once you are within the section, reviewing the Citing Decisions or Notes of Decisions will quickly alert you to cases interpreting and applying this constitutional provision. In this case, making a constitutionality argument about the jury question is likely ill-advised (*see Wheeler v. State*, 255 Ind. 395 (1970) (holding the section is inapplicable to qualification of jurors and does not prevent the state, in a prosecution for murder, from questioning the prospective jurors concerning their religious or moral beliefs which would prevent them from voting for the death penalty)).

Additionally, there are several other resources for researching federal and state constitutions worth noting. HeinOnline's "State Constitutions Illustrated" collection contains the constitutions of all fifty states, together with related documents and resources. It includes the text of every historical constitution for each state, the current texts, and documents pre-dating each jurisdictions' statehood. For Indiana, it includes original text and amendments to the Constitution of 1816 and 1851, as well as federal treaties and Indiana Territory documents. *Constitutions of the United States, National and State* is a multi-volume set containing the constitutions for the United States, each of the fifty states, and all U.S. territories. It is held by most law libraries and is particularly helpful for comparing constitutional provisions across U.S. jurisdictions. Finally, the NBER/Maryland State Constitutions Project is a free resource which provides current and historical text for each state's constitution.[1]

B. Locating and Researching the Federal Constitution

Enacted in 1789, the Constitution of the United States is the highest law in our country. It describes the structure of our federal government, including the establishment of the three independent branches of government (i.e., executive, legislative, and judicial), and the relationship between the federal government and those of the individual states. The Constitution has been amended over two dozen times in its history. Rights conferred by the U.S. Constitution cannot be curtailed by the states; however, states can guarantee additional rights beyond those bestowed by the federal constitution.

The federal constitution is published in official and unofficial versions of the United States Code (U.S.C.). Among the best resources for constitutional research are annotated codes due to the supplemental information they include. For each article, section, and clause, annotated codes contain related court decisions and suggestions for secondary sources containing commentary and analysis. An excellent resource for researching constitutional issues

---

1. Available at http://www.stateconstitutions.umd.edu/index.aspx.

is the *Constitution of the United States of America: Analysis and Interpretation* (often referred to as "Constitution Annotated"). *Constitution Annotated* is a free online resource created by the Congressional Research Service.[2] Clicking into "Browse the Constitution Annotated" takes you to a hyperlinked list of the Constitution's articles and amendments. Selecting any of them will bring up the amendment text as well as a link to a scholarly analysis tracing the history of interpretation and providing footnotes to cases and other related resources. *Constitution Annotated* also includes lists of congressional acts deemed unconstitutional and state laws determined to be unconstitutional or preempted by federal law. You can also use a treatise finder to identify additional scholarly analysis of constitutional law.[3]

II. Statutory Research

A. Introduction to Statutes

Statutes are the laws enacted by federal, state, and local legislative bodies. They are implicated in almost every legal situation you will encounter and serve many functions. Thus, when approaching a legal problem, one of the first things you need to evaluate is whether an existing statute impacts your issue. Statutes can be substantive or procedural. They are used to clarify or fill in gaps in the common law (e.g., codification of common law burglary), define responsibilities, and set forth penalties for civil and criminal offenses (e.g., establishing maximum sentences for crimes). Other statutes address issues not considered by common law. Statutes can also govern issues such as format of pleadings and time limitations. Frequently, statutes are the first primary authority you'll want to consult when handling a legal problem. If your issue is addressed by a statute, you should begin by finding and reading the statutory text. Both state and federal jurisdictions share the same publication path for statutes: from slip law to session law to the codified version, and, ultimately, to inclusion in an annotated code. Annotated codes incorporate editorial content along with the statutory text to help attorneys and other researchers understand, interpret, and apply the statute. Table 4-1 lists commonly included features in annotated codes.

---

2. Available at https://constitution.congress.gov/.
3. See Chapter 3 for more information on treatise finders and how to use them.

Table 4-1. Annotated Code Features

Feature	Function
Notes of Decisions (or Notes to Decisions)	"Notes of/to Decisions" contain topically arranged summaries of major cases (with hyperlinks to the opinions, if used electronically) that significantly interpret or apply a particular statute. On Westlaw, researchers can browse to relevant cases using the Notes' Table of Contents, or by using filters to restrict the opinions by jurisdiction, date, or Key Number.
History	Details the history of the statutory provision, including summaries of amendments as well as the public law numbers and *Statutes at Large* citations for the laws containing the revisions. It also includes cases and pending legislation that may affect the statute.
Citing References (or Citing Decisions and Other Citing Sources)	Contains references to cases interpreting the statute, administrative agency regulations implementing the statute, secondary sources, and cross-references to related statutes.
Research References & Practice Aids (or Context & Analysis)	Refers researchers to secondary sources with in-depth analysis and other significant information about the statute. Depending upon the number of references, this section is sometimes subdivided into categories (e.g., ALR library, law review and journal commentaries, encyclopedias, etc.). It also includes references to relevant topics and Key Numbers (Westlaw only) to help expand your research by leading you to additional cases on the subject.

B. Indiana Statutory Research

1. Structure of Indiana Statutes

Indiana's official state code is the *Indiana Code*. It has 36 titles. The *Indiana Code* is available both in print and online. In addition to the official, unannotated, version of the code, two unofficial annotated versions—*West's Annotated Indiana Code* and *Burns Indiana Statutes Annotated*—are also published. The annotated versions are available in Westlaw and Lexis, respectively.[4] Indiana's statutes are available in several commercial databases.

---

4. Bloomberg Law has the Indiana Code text, but with limited additional information. Its Smart Code® feature supplements state codes by identifying case decisions that cite a given statute and provides depth of discussion data, but no references to analytical materials.

Contemporary Indiana session laws are available in Lexis (i.e., Indiana Advance Legislative Service), with coverage from 1989 to present, and Westlaw (i.e., Indiana Enacted Legislation (Session Laws)), with coverage from 2016 through 2019.[5] For older acts, HeinOnline's "Session Laws Library" has the full run of Indiana sessions laws back to the state's inception, including Indiana Territory session laws from 1801 until Indiana achieved statehood in 1816. LLMC Digital also has historical Indiana session laws, with coverage from 1853 – 1990.

Case opinions clarify the meaning of statutes by analyzing and applying them to different situations. Consequently, the case opinions and regulations associated with a statute can become more meaningful sources of information than the actual text of the statutes they apply. As a solution, unofficial codes with annotations were produced. Annotations are additional information included by editors to assist researchers in interpreting, analyzing, and applying the statutory text. The statutory text itself remains the same as the official version. Annotated codes also contain a variety of finding aids to assist researchers.

If the situation you are researching happened in the past, you may need to look for a superseded code. Superseded codes are historical versions of the code. Always make sure the code you are using was in effect during the time period pertinent to your issue. For example, if your client is charged with committing a burglary in 2004, you must look at the relevant statutory provisions in force at the time of the alleged offense. For this reason, many law libraries retain older code sets. Superseded state codes are also available online in HeinOnline's "State Statutes: A Historical Archive" collection. Table 4-2 describes the Indiana state statutory publications and where to find them.

---

5. The *Indiana Legislative Service* is updated daily in Lexis.

Table 4-2. Indiana State Statutory Publications

Statutory Publication	Description	Citation Format	Sources
Session law	Chronological publication of all laws enacted during a legislative session in the *Indiana Acts.*	\<year\> Indiana Acts \<page no.\>	Lexis Westlaw HeinOnline IN General Assembly[6]
Code	Subject arrangement of Indiana public laws in effect at the time of publication.	Ind. Code § x-x-x-x (\<year\>)	*Indiana Code*
Annotated Code	Code text paired with references to interpretive cases, related regulations, and secondary sources providing analysis of its statutory provisions.	Ind. Code Ann. § x-x-x-x (West \<year\>) Ind. Code Ann. § x-x-x-x (LexisNexis \<year\>)	*West's Annotated Indiana Code* *Burns Indiana Statutes Annotated*

2. Researching Indiana Statutes in Print and Online

Ideally, your research in a secondary source will have led you to relevant statutes. If there are no secondary sources on your topic, there are other approaches to finding the statutes you need. First, generate a list of keywords based upon the facts and legal issues. If researching statutes in print, select a few of those keywords to look for in the index. When researching statutes electronically, use the terms you chose to run terms and connectors or natural language searches within the annotated codes available in either Lexis or Westlaw. Review your search results to find the statutory sections applicable to your situation. Read the statutory text of each section fully. Click into the "table of contents" to view the organization of the full statutory scheme. Review any related sections with implications for your scenario. Take

---

6. The Indiana General Assembly's website is: http://iga.in.gov/.

advantage of the annotations in the annotated code and allow them to lead you to pertinent regulations and cases interpreting and applying the statute.

There are several ways to find statutes. Table 4-3 lists the process for statutory research. The methods you choose will be determined by the information available to you and whether you are using a print or electronic resource. If you have a citation to a known code section, that is the easiest way to access a statute in print or online. Let's walk through how to find *Ind. Code* § 31-14-2-1, about how to establish paternity in a family law case. In print, you'd find the volume containing the Title (e.g., Title 31: Family Law and Juvenile Law), look for the Article (e.g., Article 14: Establishment of Paternity), then the Chapter (e.g., Chapter 2: Methods of Establishing Paternity), and finally the section (e.g., Sec. 1: Exclusive methods of establishing paternity).

If you did not know the citation and were using a print code, another way of finding the relevant code section would be to use the finding aids incorporated into the publication. Here, the table of contents, subject index, and popular names table would be useful for steering you towards the right spot in the code. For example, you would likely search for "paternity" in the index. You'd discover that it is an entry in the index, but that it refers you to a different index heading, "Children Born Out of Wedlock." Underneath that phrase in the index is a list of several dozen subtopics. Among them is an entry for "Methods of Establishing: In ST 31-14-2-1" which directs you to the proper code section.

An advantage to doing statutory research online is the ability to run full-text searches in the code. The major commercial databases support natural language, terms and connectors, and segment searching within federal and state codes.[7]

3. Reading and Updating Statutes

The terminology of a statute is exclusive to each statutory scheme. Don't assume that the layman's definition is controlling. Always look for a definitions section when researching in statutes, because that dictates how specific words are used in that particular statutory construct. For example, in the Fair Housing Act, "dwelling" is defined as "any building, structure, or portion thereof which is occupied as, or designed or intended for occupancy as, a residence by one or more families, and any vacant land which is offered for sale

---

7. Read Chapter 2 covering research tools and strategies and use the information there to optimize your statutory research.

Table 4-3. Process for Statutory Research

Recommended Steps
1. **Generate a list of keywords and terms.** Use the techniques covered in Chapter 2 (e.g., "journalists' questions" or the TARPP method). When compiling your list, use synonyms and think of broad terms (e.g., "fruit" instead of "apple").
2. **Search the index for your terms** (if searching in print or using an electronic resource with an index).
3. **Browse the table of contents.** This technique has the added benefit of apprising the researcher of the substance of surrounding sections, allowing you to get a better sense of the overall statutory scheme.
4. **Read the statute.** Also read any sections referred to by your original section and look at the historical notes to ensure that you are looking at the section in force during the relevant time period.
5. **Locate and read related provisions.** Check the provisions immediately surrounding your original section as they are usually interrelated and intended to be applied together. Depending upon your issue, look for "penalty" provisions and "definitions" sections for that portion of the code.
6. **Update the code sections.** Use a citator (or, if researching in print, pocket parts and supplements) to verify the validity of all provisions you intend to rely on.

or lease for the construction or location thereon of any such building, structure, or portion thereof."[8] That definition is only valid for that Act. Other statutes using the term "dwelling" may have alternate definitions or may use the term without specifically defining it.

For a given research problem, it is likely that you will need to apply multiple statutory provisions. Don't stop searching because you've found one as there may be other sections relevant to your issue. Once you've found an applicable statute, you need to verify it is still in effect and hasn't been amended or repealed. This process is referred to as "updating" the statute. In print, check the pocket part in the back of the volume or its cumulative supplement. These updating materials are produced at the conclusion of each legislative session and let you know about newly enacted legislation and any changes in existing laws. If you're using an annotated code, it will also apprise you of any new cases, secondary sources, research references, etc., that have been added to that section. Always pay attention to the dates on the pocket parts, supplements, and legislative service pamphlets that you use to update the statute.

---

8. 42 U.S.C. § 3602.

Avoid common pitfalls when doing statutory research. Always look for related or cross-referenced code sections. Do this by using the table of contents to scan the sections immediately surrounding your target section(s) and reviewing those that may be relevant to your research. Also, read all sections referred to by your code section. Read the statutory text carefully. Take your time and don't assume that the statute's title alone fully captures its content or applicability. Be mindful that there may be statutorily defined terms used, and refer to the definitions section governing the statutory scheme to interpret the text. Finally, never fail to update the statutes you've found. In print, check the pocket parts and supplements every time. Electronically, consult the currency note and use a citator (e.g., KeyCite or Shepard's) to verify that every section you rely upon is still in force.

C. Federal Statutory Research

When Congress passes a bill into law, it is first published in a form called a "slip law." At the conclusion of each Congressional session, that session's slip laws are organized chronologically by date of passage and bound into volumes called the *United States Statutes at Large*. These are referred to as "session laws" because they are published at the end of the legislative session. Session laws are then organized by subject and incorporated into the *United States Code* through a process called codification.

The *United States Code* (U.S.C.) is the official federal code. Its topical organization makes it far easier to do research than the cumbersome chronological structure of the *Statutes at Large*. The *United States Code* was first published in 1926. Currently, it has 54 titles, each covering a broad subject. In print, new versions are published every six years and, in the intervening years, it is updated annually with cumulative supplements.[9] The official version of the code is "unannotated," meaning that it contains only the statutory text and limited historical notes. There is no other information included to assist attorneys, judges, and other legal professionals in interpreting and applying its statutory provisions. This is problematic because the meaning of a statute is often facially unclear and, thus, the statutory language must be construed by the courts.

If you know the name of an Act (e.g., the Affordable Care Act) and want to find where it has been codified, use the Popular Names Table in print or

---

9. Subject to a publication lag of approximately 2 years.

electronically. A complete list of U.S.C.'s titles is included in a table of contents in the print publication and online. If you know the title or general subject matter of a statute (e.g., copyright) you can browse to the title (e.g., Title 17: Copyrights) and look through its chapters and their sections to find relevant statutes. Table 4-4 details the federal statutory publications.

Table 4-4. Federal Statutory Publications

Statutory Publication	Description	Citation Format & Example	Sources
Slip law	Single legislative act printed on paper in a pamphlet-like format. Slip laws are the first official publication of a newly passed law. Each contains the title of the act, the statutory text, and helpful marginalia, including notes about where different sections will be codified in the *United States Code*.	**Pub. L. No.** **<Cong. session enacted>** **- <sequentially assigned # based upon when the law passed>** e.g., Pub. L. No. 94 - 553	Lexis [*USCS*—Public Laws] Westlaw United States Public laws (2013 –) United States Public Laws Historical (1973 – 2012) Congress.gov public laws (1973 –) Govinfo.gov public and private laws (1995 –)
Session law	Chronological publication of all laws enacted during a legislative session in the *United States Statutes at Large*.	**<volume> Stat.** **<page #>** e.g., 90 Stat. 2541	Lexis Westlaw HeinOnline Congress.gov (1973–) Govinfo.gov
Code	Subject-based arrangement of all United States public laws in effect at the time of publication.	**<title> USC §** **<section>** e.g., 17 USC § 101	*United States Code*
Annotated Code	Statutory code text paired with references to interpretive cases, related regulations, and secondary sources providing analysis of its statutory provisions.	**<title> USCA §** **<section>** **<title> USCS §** **<section>** e.g., 17 USCA §101	*United States Code Annotated* (*USCA*) *United States Code Service* (*USCS*)

There are two annotated versions of the United States Code: *United States Code Annotated* (U.S.C.A.) by Thomson West and *United States Code Service* (U.S.C.S.) published by LexisNexis. In addition to the statutory text, these publications include other primary sources such as the U.S. Constitution and federal court rules. The organization of both annotated codes is identical to that of the official *United States Code*; however, the U.S.C.S. uses the statutory language as it appears in the *Statutes at Large*, whereas U.S.C.A.'s statutory text is identical to that of the U.S.C. There are also differences between the annotations in the U.S.C.S. and U.S.C.A. For example, different interpretive cases are included—the U.S.C.A. strives to be comprehensive in its case annotations; in contrast, U.S.C.S. annotations are selective and editorially-determined. References to secondary sources also tend to be publisher-specific (i.e., Westlaw suggests consulting other Thomson West publications and Lexis includes references to LexisNexis works). Refer back to Table 4-1, Annotated Code Features, for descriptions of the major tools included in U.S.C.A. and U.S.C.S. While annotated codes are superior for doing legal research, you always want to cite to the official version of the code. Proper citation to a statute requires the title, code abbreviation, and section number.

III. Court Rules

Court rules set forth the procedures for conducting business in the courts. These rules touch on such issues as time limitations, pleadings allowed, grounds for appeal, as well as more granular matters like font and format of pleadings, courtroom attire, and even hours for court personnel. Overall, court rules aim to help the court run in a manner that is efficient, routine, and predictable for litigants and their attorneys. Court rules include statutorily prescribed procedural rules as well as those of individual courts.

The process by which court rules are created varies by jurisdiction and, typically, involves action from both the legislative and judicial branches. Federal and state legislatures pass statutes broadly covering these issues and authorize the courts to fill in any gaps that may exist.[10] The Supreme Court of the United States creates generally applicable court rules[11] for itself and the

---

10. Indiana's Supreme Court has the statutory authority to promulgate court rules for its state courts (*see* I.C. § 34-8-1-3).

11. The general court rules for the federal judiciary are the Federal Rules of Civil Procedure (F.R.C.P.), Federal Rules of Criminal Procedure (F.R. Crim. P.), Federal

lower federal courts. Lower federal courts (i.e., federal courts of appeals and district courts) can make additional rules for themselves, provided those rules are not inconsistent with the general rules. Specialty courts, such as bankruptcy, also promulgate their own rules. Court rules are customarily published alongside state and federal statutory codes.[12] You can identify court rules by name, as they are usually referred to as "rules of procedure" or "rules of court."

Always use an annotated code to research court rules as they contain valuable supplemental information that will help you understand and apply the rules. Due to similarities in the organization of statutes and court rules, the same techniques and strategies used for statutory research are effective for these rules as well.

A. Indiana Court Rules

Indiana Rules of Court can be found in print and online. The process for finding court rules is outlined in Table 4-5. One of the best places to find the text of current local rules is on court websites. Indiana's judicial branch publishes rules for the state courts[13] as well as local rules for each of Indiana's counties[14] on its website. State court websites for all fifty states are linked on the National Center for State Courts' "State Court Websites" page.[15] Annotated versions of Indiana court rules are available in Lexis[16] and Westlaw.[17] Regardless of the source, always look for and note how current the rules you have found are. This information is usually shown at the beginning of the set of rules, or through a nearby hyperlink to the rules, with the designation "current as of" or "last updated" on a given date.

Rules of Appellate Procedure (F.R. App. P.), and the Federal Rules of Evidence (F.R.E.).

12. Bloomberg Law, Lexis, and Westlaw have court rules for all fifty states.

13. The website is https://www.in.gov/courts/publications/rules/.

14. The website is https://www.in.gov/courts/publications/local-rules/.

15. The website is https://www.ncsc.org/information-and-resources/state-court-websites.

16. In the collection IN — Indiana Local, State & Federal Court Rules.

17. In the Indiana collection, under the header Statutes & Court Rules.

Table 4-5. Process for Court Rules Research

1. Identify the jurisdiction(s) and the type of action (e.g., civil or criminal)
2. Locate all applicable sets of court rules (general, specialized, and local)
3. Scan the table of contents
4. Fully read all relevant rules
5. Check to see if there have been any changes to the rules either by court order or amendment.
6. Act accordingly!

Procedural rules come into play at every stage of litigation. Be aware that multiple sets of rules may apply to a single proceeding. For example, if you were representing a client in connection with a burglary charge in Bloomington, Indiana, you would want to consult at least three different sets of court rules: Indiana's Rules of Criminal Procedure, Indiana's Rules of Evidence, and the local rules for Monroe County. Depending upon the particular circumstances of the case, you may even need to research additional rule sets, such as Jury Rules or Post-Conviction Remedies.

A common mistake made when researching court rules is not paying close enough attention to the details. Always read the rule very carefully and be sure to look for, consult, and read any and all cross-references to other rules or statutes. Often a single action involves several different court rules. Take your time and make sure that you have found all of the controlling rules and guidance. Don't ignore "inconvenient" rules. Times and circumstances will arise where it would seem advantageous for you or your client if you did not follow the court's rules. Fail to follow the court rules at your own peril—don't assume it will go unnoticed. In a litigation context, there is no better way to reveal that you are a novice than to ignore the court rules. Conversely, being well-versed in your jurisdiction's court rules will inspire confidence in your work from your supervisors, partners, and clients.

B. Federal Court Rules

In the U.S.C. and U.S.C.A., the federal rules appear in the appendix to Title 28: Judiciary and Judicial Procedure, except for the Federal Rules of Criminal Procedure, which are appended to Title 18: Crimes and Criminal Procedure. In contrast, the U.S.C.S. separates court rules from the main body of the code, providing them in discrete volumes at the end of the set and as a standalone collection in Lexis (e.g., Statutes & Legislation > Court Rules).

One of the best places to find the text of current local rules is on court websites.[18] Use the Administrative Office of the U.S. Courts' Federal Court Finder to find information about specific federal courts by searching by location or court name.[19] Once on the court's site, look for content related to "rules" or "attorneys." For example, the local rules for the U.S. District Court for the Southern District of Indiana are prominently linked under "Local Rules and Court Orders" on its website.[20]

Secondary sources can assist you in understanding and following court rules. Most of these resources provide the text of the rule followed by an analysis of its effects and citations to case opinions that have applied the rule. The two major procedural treatises are *Wright & Miller's Federal Practice and Procedure* (Thomson West) and *Moore's Federal Practice* (LexisNexis). Each of these treatises is organized by federal rule and contains an explanation of rules and how they have been applied, with citations to illustrative cases. Form books,[21] your law firm's document banks, and previously filed court documents (e.g., pleadings, motions, etc.) can also serve as examples of how the court rules operate. However, exercise caution: simply because a document has been filed in a case doesn't mean it is compliant with the rules or is of high quality.

There are several methods of finding judicial opinions construing the federal rules. In Lexis and Westlaw, you can identify cases discussing and applying a rule by using Shepard's or KeyCite. Retrieve the rule for which you want to locate case law and use the "Notes of/to Decisions" to find cases that significantly analyze it. Thomson West also publishes all U.S. District Court cases interpreting any federal civil or criminal procedural rule in its *Federal Rules Decisions* reporter. Similarly, cases interpreting the Civil and Appellate Procedure rules are collected and published in the *Federal Rules Service* (LexisNexis).

---

18. Federal courts are required to publish their court's rules on their websites.

19. The website is https://www.uscourts.gov/.

20. The website is https://www.insd.uscourts.gov/court-info/local-rules-and -orders.

21. Federal and state formbooks contain model forms which usually conform to the jurisdiction's court rules.

Chapter 5

Court Structure and Judicial Opinions

The United States is a *common law* jurisdiction, meaning that, in the absence of a statute or regulation governing a legal issue, judges can create law through the cases they decide. This common law is found in judicial decisions, or case opinions, published in chronological series called *reporters.* Some courts have their own reporter that publishes cases from that court alone; other common reporters cover several courts within a defined geographic region; still others cover particular types of cases, such as tax or bankruptcy. It is important to familiarize yourself with these print reporters, because even when conducting online research, case citations reference the print. This chapter begins with a brief overview of the Indiana and federal court systems, followed by a discussion of the different types of case reporters, and ending with advice on how to analyze a court opinion.

I. Court Systems

At both the state and federal level, court systems are generally divided into three tiers: trial court, intermediate appellate court, and final appellate court.

A. Indiana Courts

The Indiana Constitution establishes three types of courts in the state: The Indiana Supreme Court, the Indiana Court of Appeals, and circuit courts. These are commonly known as constitutional courts and can only be abolished by constitutional amendment.[1] This same article of the Indiana Constitution provides for "such other courts as the General Assembly may establish."[2] These are known as legislative courts and can be abolished by the

---

1. Ind. Const. Art. VII, § 1.
2. *Id.*

General Assembly at any time. Examples of legislative courts in Indiana include the Indiana Tax Court, superior courts, and city and town courts. Table 5-1 demonstrates the three-tier court system in Indiana.

Table 5-1. Indiana Court Structure

Level of Court	Indiana Court Designation		
Final Appellate Level	Indiana Supreme Court		
Intermediate Appellate Level	Indiana Court of Appeals	Indiana Tax Court	
Trial Level	Circuit Courts	Superior Courts	City and Town Courts

Trial courts in Indiana include city and town courts, circuit courts, and superior courts; intermediate appellate courts include the Indiana Court of Appeals and the Indiana Tax Court; and the final appellate court is the Indiana Supreme Court. The different types of Indiana trial courts have similar responsibilities. City and town courts have the most limited jurisdiction, handling cases concerning violations of municipal ordinances, misdemeanors, and other infractions. Per the Indiana Constitution, every county in Indiana has a circuit court, most of which have original jurisdiction in all civil and criminal cases, unless an exception has been conferred by law for a particular jurisdiction. Superior courts have concurrent jurisdiction with circuit courts. While every county in Indiana has a circuit court, whether a county also includes a city, town, or superior court varies by county. Monroe County, for example, has only a circuit court, while Carroll County has circuit, superior, and city courts.[3] Marion County has the state's only small claims courts, and St. Joseph County has the state's only probate court.[4]

With few exceptions,[5] trial court cases in Indiana can be appealed to the Indiana Court of Appeals. Fifteen judges serve the Indiana Court of Appeals,

---

3. The court directory on the Indiana Courts website is a helpful tool for determining each county's local court structure: https://www.in.gov/courts/local/.

4. In the absence of a separate court for small claims or probate issues, circuit and superior courts hear these cases as a part of their general jurisdiction. Allen County, for example, has magistrate judges that hear probate and small claims cases; and Marion County has several subject-specific superior courts, one of which has jurisdiction over probate issues.

5. Cases that do not appeal to the Indiana Court of Appeals include: cases where the verdict includes the death penalty or life without parole (appealed directly to the

but they do not preside simultaneously over the same case; rather each case heard by the Indiana Court of Appeals is presided over by a rotating three-judge panel. The Indiana Tax Court takes appeals of any cases involving state tax law; unlike the Indiana Court of Appeals, the Indiana Tax Court has only one judge who oversees all tax cases. Both courts are located in the Indiana Statehouse in Indianapolis, but the Tax Court will also, if elected by the taxpayer, hear cases in Allen, Jefferson, Lake, Marion, St. Joseph, Vanderburgh, and Vigo counties.[6]

The Indiana Supreme Court is the final appellate court for issues pertaining to state law. Even if a case that involved both state and federal law were appealed to the Supreme Court of the United States, the justices would only rule on matters of federal law, deferring to the Indiana Supreme Court for state law matters. The Indiana Supreme Court consists of one chief justice and four associate justices. The court is located in Indianapolis. This court has original jurisdiction in matters pertaining to admission to the practice of law, attorney and judge discipline, and the unauthorized practice of law. In addition to the limited direct trial court appeals (see footnote 5), the Indiana Supreme Court may review decisions of the Indiana Court of Appeals or the Indiana Tax Court.

B. Other State Court Systems

Most states follow a similar three-tier system, but there are some anomalies. For example, Texas has two final appellate courts; the Texas Supreme Court hears final appeals of state civil matters, and the Texas Court of Criminal Appeals hears final appeals of state criminal matters. Likewise, the nomenclature for the final appellate court can differ. In New York, supreme courts are trial courts, while the final appellate court is known as the New York Court of Appeals. It is important to understand the court structure for a jurisdiction when conducting legal research. Court structure charts can be found online in a number of places;[7] another helpful source is the set of jurisdictional tables at the back of the *Bluebook*.

Indiana Supreme Court); cases in which the trial court rules that a statute is unconstitutional (appealed directly to the Indiana Supreme Court); cases involving attorney discipline (appealed directly to the Indiana Supreme Court); and cases involving taxation (appealed to the Indiana Tax Court). *See* https://www.in.gov/courts/appeals/about/.

6. *See* https://www.in.gov/courts/tax/about/.

7. The Indiana Court Structure can be found on the Indiana Courts website, https://www.in.gov/courts/about/. The Court Statistics Project of the National Center

C. Federal Courts

At the federal level, trial courts are called United States District Courts; intermediate appellate courts are United States Courts of Appeals, and the final appellate court is the Supreme Court of the United States. Table 5-2 shows the three-tier federal court structure, with specific examples for cases originating in Indiana.

Table 5-2. Federal Court Structure

Level of Court	Federal Designation	Indiana Federal Jurisdiction	
Final Appellate Level	United States Supreme Court	United States Supreme Court	
Intermediate Appellate Level	United States Courts of Appeals	U.S. Court of Appeals for the Seventh Circuit	
Trial Level	United States District Courts	U.S. District Court, Northern District of Indiana	U.S. District Court, Southern District of Indiana

Each state has at least one U.S. District Court, determined by population and caseload. As seen in Table 5-2, Indiana is divided into two federal court districts. The U.S. District Court for the Northern District of Indiana governs federal trial cases in the upper third of the state, where the population is densest, with locations in Fort Wayne, Hammond, Lafayette, and South Bend. The U.S. District Court for the Southern District of Indiana governs federal trial cases in roughly the lower two-thirds of the state, with locations in Indianapolis, Terre Haute, Evansville, and New Albany.

At the intermediate appellate level, the country is divided into twelve geo-graphically-defined circuits, eleven numerical (First through Eleventh) and the District of Columbia. Indiana is in the Seventh Circuit, with Illinois and Wisconsin. A thirteenth federal circuit, known simply as the Federal Circuit,

---

for State Courts maintains court structure charts for all fifty states, Guam, and Puerto Rico, https://www.courtstatistics.org/state_court_structure_charts. At the federal level, a good explanation and chart of federal district and circuit courts can be found on the website of the Administrative Office of the U.S. Courts, https://www.uscourts.gov/about-federal-courts/court-role-and-structure.

hears district court appeals pertaining to certain legal subjects, including patents, trademarks, government contracts, and veterans' benefits, as well as appeals from other specialized courts and certain administrative agencies.[8]

The final appellate level for cases involving federal statutes or the United States Constitution is the Supreme Court of the United States, comprised of one chief justice and eight associate justices. The Supreme Court has discretion over which cases it will hear; parties wishing to appeal their case to the Supreme Court must first file a petition for *certiorari* to make this request.

II. Judicial Opinions

Judicial decisions, or case opinions, are published in a three-step process: first, the court publishes the case as a *slip opinion*, a slim publication containing just the text of the case opinion. Today, many courts publish their slip opinions on their website as well as in print.[9] Once several slip opinions from cases have been published, the court binds those slip opinions together into a small paperback publication known as an *advance sheet*. Likewise, once several advance sheets have been issued, the court further collects these into a hardbound volume called a *reporter*. Reporters are chronological publications of cases from a particular jurisdiction, court, or geographical region, or pertaining to a particular subject.

Historically, courts themselves published their case opinions; as time went on, several commercial reporters began production as well, which led to jurisdictions having both official and unofficial reporters. In reality, there is little difference between a case as reported in an official versus an unofficial reporter. Unofficial reporters can have great advantages, in fact, such as editorial enhancements that are helpful to the reader; however, if the language in a case opinion differs between an official and an unofficial reporter, the official is the most reliable version.[10]

---

8. *See* https://cafc.uscourts.gov/home/the-court/about-the-court/court-jurisdic -tion/.

9. Slip opinions from the Indiana Supreme Court, Court of Appeals, and Tax Court are available back to 2017 at https://public.courts.in.gov/decisions?c=9510. Slip opinions of the United States Supreme Court are available back to 2014 at https:// www.supremecourt.gov/opinions/slipopinion/20.

10. Jurisdictional tables at the back of the *Bluebook* can help you determine which reporter is the official publication for your jurisdiction.

A. Indiana

Many courts have ceased publication of their own reporters and have instead designated a particular commercial reporter as their official reporter. In Indiana, the *North Eastern Reporter*, published by Thomson West, is the official reporter of cases from the Indiana Supreme Court, Indiana Court of Appeals, and the Indiana Tax Court. Prior to this, there were three Indiana reporters: *Blackford's Reports of Cases*, publishing Indiana Supreme Court decisions from 1817 to 1847; this transitioned to *Indiana Reports*, which published Indiana Supreme Court decisions from 1848 to 1981. Cases from the Indiana Appellate Court (now the Indiana Court of Appeals) were published in *Indiana Appellate Court Reports* from 1890 to 1972 and the *Indiana Court of Appeals Reports* from 1973 to 1979. State trial level courts do not issue written opinions.

B. Regional Reporters

The most robust system of reporters in the United States are West's regional reporters, a system of commercial reporters that began publication in the 1800s. The West Publishing Company divided the country into a series of broad regions, and each regional reporter publishes cases from several states within that region. Refer to Table 5-3 for more information on these reporters.

Table 5-3. West's Regional Reporters

Reporter Name and Abbreviation	States Covered
Atlantic Reporter (A., A.2d, A.3d)	Connecticut, Delaware, District of Columbia, Maine, Maryland, New Hampshire, New Jersey, Pennsylvania, Rhode Island, Vermont
North Eastern Reporter (N.E., N.E.2d, N.E.3d)	Illinois, Indiana, Massachusetts, New York, Ohio
North Western Reporter (N.W., N.W.2d)	Iowa, Michigan, Minnesota, Nebraska, North Dakota, South Dakota, Wisconsin
Pacific Reporter (P., P.2d, P.3d)	Alaska, Arizona, California, Colorado, Hawaii, Idaho, Kansas, Montana, Nevada, New Mexico, Oklahoma, Oregon, Utah, Washington, Wyoming

South Eastern Reporter (S.E., S.E.2d)	Georgia, North Carolina, South Carolina, Virginia, West Virginia
South Western Reporter (S.W., S.W.2d, S.W.3d)	Arkansas, Kentucky, Missouri, Tennessee, Texas
Southern Reporter (So., So.2d, So.3d)	Alabama, Florida, Louisiana, Mississippi

If some of these states seem misplaced (for example, few people would think of Indiana as "north eastern"), keep in mind that these were arbitrary groupings, initially established in the 1800s, when the country looked markedly different. It is also important to remember that the regional reporters are for state cases, so they do not correspond with the federal circuits that states are separately grouped into. For instance, Indiana is in the Seventh Circuit with Illinois and Wisconsin, but Indiana and Illinois state cases are published in the *North Eastern Reporter*, while Wisconsin state cases are published in the *North Western Reporter*. Federal reporters will be covered in the next section.

Note the abbreviations in Table 5-3. Reporters are published in series. The *North Eastern Reporter* began publication in 1885 with its first series (N.E.). In 1936, series two began (N.E.2d). The reporter is now in its third series (N.E.3d), begun in 1988. Each series of a reporter is a continuation of the last, so if you come across a citation to a case in the first series (N.E.) and wanted to locate the case in a print reporter, you would need to find the volumes of the *North Eastern Reporter*, first series, as this case will not be reproduced in series two or three.

C. Citing Cases

Citations to cases in reporters can seem confusing at first, but are formulaic and easy to follow, once you understand the elements. Take, for example, the case of *Hess v. State*, a freedom of speech case. The citation to the Indiana Supreme Court opinion in this case is 297 N.E.2d 413 (Ind. 1973). Each element of this citation informs you how to find the case in a reporter. See Table 5-4 for an explanation of what each element refers to.

Table 5-4. Elements of a Case Citation

Hess v. State	297	N.E.2d	413	(Ind.[11]	1973).
Party Names	Reporter Volume	2nd series of the *North Eastern Reporter*	Starting page number in the volume	Deciding court (Indiana Supreme Court)	Year of decision

Often a case will have multiple citations, called *parallel citations*, if it has been published in more than one reporter. *Hess v. State*, for example, was also published in *Indiana Reports*, the former official reporter for Indiana Supreme Court cases, which has since ceased publication. Its citation to *Hess v. State* is 260 Ind. 427 (1973). Following the same rules for reading a case citation, you now know that 260 is the volume number where you would find this case in *Indiana Reports*, starting at page 427. When you come across a case with parallel citations, the geographical tables in the back of the *Bluebook* are a helpful resource for determining which to cite to. For this case, for instance, although at the time *Indiana Reports* was the official reporter for the state of Indiana, the *Bluebook* directs you to cite to the *North Eastern Reporter* for any Indiana Supreme Court cases since 1885.[12]

III. Federal Reporters

At the federal level, a number of official and unofficial case reporters exist, as shown in Table 5-5.

---

11. Recall that the regional reporters, such as the *North Eastern Reporter*, contain cases from several states' intermediate and final appellate courts. Thus in the parenthetical at the end of the case citation, they include a description of the court. *Ind.* stands for Indiana Supreme Court. *Ind. App.* stands for Indiana Court of Appeals.

12. *The Bluebook: A Uniform System of Citation* tbl.T.1.3 Indiana (Columbia L. Rev. Ass'n et. al. eds., 21st ed. 2021).

Table 5-5. Federal Case Reporters

Court	Reporter	Abbreviation	Official Reporter
United States Supreme Court	*United States Reports* *Supreme Court Reporter* *United States Supreme Court Reports, Lawyers' Edition*	U.S. S. Ct. L. Ed., L. Ed. 2d	*United States Reports*
United States Courts of Appeals	*Federal Reporter*	F., F.2d, F.3d, F.4th	Slip Opinion
United States District Courts	*Federal Supplement*	F. Supp, F. Supp. 2d	Slip Opinion

A. United States Supreme Court Cases

For the Supreme Court of the United States, the official reporter is the *United States Reports*, published by the court itself. In addition, Thomson West publishes the *Supreme Court Reporter*, and Michie (LexisNexis) publishes *U.S. Supreme Court Reports, Lawyers' Edition*. As the official reporter, if possible, cite to the *United States Reports*. However, this publication is typically several years behind schedule; therefore, as needed, most lawyers will cite to *Supreme Court Reporter*. In addition, the slip opinions for the court's decisions from 2014 to present are available on the court's website.[13]

B. United States Courts of Appeals and United States District Courts

For United States Courts of Appeals and United States District Courts, the official report of a case is the slip opinion; the courts do not publish official reporters. However, several commercial reporters publish unofficial versions of the case opinions. West's *Federal Reporter* covers published decisions of the thirteen federal circuits. West's *Federal Supplement* publishes select U.S.

---

13. Find US Supreme Court slip opinions at https://www.supremecourt.gov/opinions/slipopinion/21.

District Court opinions. From 2001–2021, West's *Federal Appendix* published unreported decisions not published in the *Federal Reporter*.[14]

C. Topical Reporters

In addition to reporters that cover specific jurisdictions, many commercial reporters cover specific types of cases. For example, West's *Federal Rules Decisions* covers cases from the U.S. District Courts that specifically deal with procedural issues under the *Federal Rules of Civil Procedure* and the *Federal Rules of Criminal Procedure*. You can also find commercial reporters specific to subjects such as bankruptcy, veterans' appeals, and military justice.

D. Published v. Unpublished Opinions

Not all cases a court decides are designated for publication. The court itself makes this determination, typically opting for cases that move the law forward in some meaningful way, such as expanding existing law to fit a new factual scenario, overturning existing precedent, or calling into question the constitutionality of a statute. Opinions that are designated for publication are commonly referred to as *published* or *reported* opinions; and those that are not are deemed *unpublished* or *unreported*. In print, these designations made sense; but databases such as Lexis and Westlaw are increasingly making these unpublished/unreported decisions available to researchers, in essence publishing an unpublished opinion. These unpublished opinions have no precedential value; and whether you can even cite to an unpublished opinion varies by jurisdiction. For those who allow it, you would cite to an unpublished opinion as persuasive authority only. This can be helpful if you have found an unpublished opinion that is factually similar to your research scenario, for instance; while the precedent on your legal issue rests with another case, the application of that precedent to the factually similar unpublished opinion may be a strong persuasive measure in your legal argument. To determine whether you can cite to an unpublished opinion in your jurisdiction, refer to your jurisdiction's court rules.[15]

---

14. More on unpublished decisions later in this chapter.

15. In Indiana, Rule of Appellate Procedure 65 dictates that all Indiana Supreme Court cases are published, as well as select Indiana Court of Appeals cases. For those Court of Appeals cases not selected for publication, Rule 65(D) states these unpublished memorandum decisions are not to be cited, unless a party is citing it on the

IV. Online Access to Cases

Now that you have an understanding of how cases are published in print, this section will discuss a variety of online sources, beyond Lexis and West-law, where state and federal case law can be accessed. Commercial databases like Lexis and Westlaw have significant bodies of case law at both the state and federal levels. These databases offer other enhancements as well, such as the inclusion of unreported decisions, as well as research tools that can help the researcher find related cases and ensure that a case they have found is still good law. These tools will be discussed in greater detail in the next chapter.

Commercial databases, however, can be expensive. Luckily, today many websites offer access to case law for free. These sites lack the editorial embellishments of commercial databases, offering simply the text of the case. For many jurisdictions, especially state courts, the coverage is more recent; therefore, access to historical cases may be limited. There are far too many sites to enumerate comprehensively here, but the following are highlights.

A. Court Websites

First and foremost, if you are looking for a recent opinion from a court, often today you will find it on the court's website. The Indiana Courts website offers a short archive of decisions from the Indiana Supreme Court, the Indiana Court of Appeals, and the Indiana Tax Court.[16] The United States Supreme Court, by comparison, in addition to recent cases, continues to add historical opinions to its website, currently back to 1991.[17]

B. Justia

Justia is a website designed to aid non-lawyers in finding answers to their legal questions. It provides access to a large body of U.S. case law. Justia has opinions of the U.S. Supreme Court from 1759 to present; the U.S. Courts of

---

grounds of res judicata, collateral estoppel, or to establish the law of the case. *See* https://w,ww.in.gov/courts/rules/appellate/index.html#_Toc60037380. For more on researching court rules, refer back to Chapter 4.

16. Indiana Judicial Branch, Appellate Decisions, https://www.in.gov/courts/public-records/appellate-decisions/.

17. United States Supreme Court, Opinions of the Court, https://www.supremecourt.gov/opinions/slipopinion/21.

Appeals and U.S. District Courts from 1924 to present; and most state appellate court decisions back to 1950.[18]

C. Findlaw

Similar to Justia, Findlaw, owned by Thomson Reuters, is a website designed to help non-lawyers find answers to their legal questions.[19] Uniquely, they have a secondary site for legal professionals that offers a wider array of legal resources.[20] Here, they provide access to U.S. Supreme Court cases back to 1760,[21] U.S. Courts of Appeals and District Courts back to 1995,[22] and state courts generally back to 1997.[23]

D. Google Scholar

Google Scholar is best known for researching journal articles from a variety of disciplines, but Google has also amassed a vast database of case law.[24] To search cases instead of articles, simply select the "Cases" radio button below the search bar. Google Scholar provides access to U.S. Supreme Court cases back to 1791, U.S. Courts of Appeals and District Court cases back to 1923, and states generally back to 1950.

Apart from the vast case law coverage it provides, another feature that sets Google Scholar apart is its "How Cited" feature, which provides the reader with snippets from later cases that cited to that particular case, offering the reader an idea of how later cases treated that case.

---

18. Justia, U.S. Case Law, https://law.justia.com/cases/.

19. Findlaw, https://www.findlaw.com/.

20. Findlaw for Legal Professionals, https://lp.findlaw.com/.

21. Findlaw, United States Supreme Court Cases, https://caselaw.findlaw.com/court/us-supreme-court. The earliest U.S. Supreme Court case was from 1791. The cases prior to 1791 that Findlaw includes in their Supreme Court collection are actually decisions of early Pennsylvania courts, dating to the colonial era, which were reprinted in the first and second volumes of the *United States Reports*.

22. Findlaw, Browse Cases and Codes, https://caselaw.findlaw.com/.

23. *Id.*

24. Google Scholar, https://scholar.google.com/.

V. Components of a Case

The heart of a reported case is the language of the opinion itself; but there are additional components to a case opinion, many added by the editors of the reporter, that are meant as an aid to the reader. These components are fairly standard from reporter to reporter. Take our case from earlier, *Hess v. State*, as an example. Please access this case online to help you visualize the following features.

A. Parallel Citations

As noted earlier, when you pull up *Hess v. State* on Lexis or Westlaw, you will see two citations at the top of the case, one from the *North Eastern Reporter* and one from *Indiana Reports*. These are referred to as *parallel citations*.

B. Parties and Procedural Designations

All parties to the case are listed next, with their procedural designation, such as plaintiff and defendant. Since the majority of opinions you read are appellate opinions, it is worth noting two additional designations. The party that appeals a case decision is generally referred to as the *appellant*, and the opposing party will be the *respondent* or the *appellee*.

C. Docket Number

When a case is filed with a court, it is assigned a unique identifier known as the docket number. This number is printed on all documents filed by the parties and the court throughout the duration of the case. For *Hess v. State*, the docket number is 1271S372. As you research a case, if you would like to look at any of these court filings, with most cases, you will need to contact the court itself to request access; this most commonly comes with an associated fee. Increasingly, jurisdictions have moved to e-filing for cases, and with that move, many courts have begun making these docket materials available on the court's website.[25]

---

25. For federal court cases in particular, you may be able to access court filings with PACER, Public Access to Court Electronic Records, https://pacer.uscourts.gov/. Anyone can create a PACER account, but be advised that accessing documents on PACER comes with a fee. Instead, if you have access to Bloomberg Law, you might try its docket search first; any filings accessed by PACER users are made available in

D. Deciding Court and Date of Decision

The preliminary case information also includes the date of the decision and the deciding court; both of these pieces of information are important for citation purposes. For example, in *Hess v. State*, the case was decided on May 22, 1973, by the Indiana Supreme Court. When citing the case, as noted in the citation section earlier in this chapter, the case is cited to the *North Eastern Reporter*, which requires identification of the court. The Indiana Supreme Court is abbreviated to "Ind." For the date, only the year is used.

E. Synopsis

When conducting case law research, the synopsis to a case can be a time-saving tool. The *synopsis*, or *case summary*, provides a quick background on the case, focusing on the main legal issues, the procedural posture, and the holding. The synopsis is provided by the publisher of the reporter, and as such, cannot be cited; but reading through the synopsis to a case can help you determine whether the case is relevant to your research, before you dive into the full opinion.

F. Disposition

At the end of the synopsis is the *disposition*, the court's decision to affirm, remand, reverse, or vacate the lower court's holding. It is also possible for the court to affirm part of a lower court's decision and reverse or remand another.

G. Headnotes

Headnotes are brief summaries (or direct quotes from the case) that identify each issue of law discussed in the case. Headnotes are described in greater detail in the next chapter. Headnotes are an editorial enhancement to the case and therefore cannot be cited as authority. When analyzing a list of cases for further research, however, headnotes, like the synopsis, can be helpful aids in assessing whether a particular case is worthy of greater attention (i.e., does it involve the legal issues you are researching?).

Bloomberg Law's docket database. Academic accountholders with Bloomberg Law also have an annual docket charge allowance that can aid the researcher in accessing court filings that are otherwise unavailable. Lexis and Westlaw also offer limited docket coverage. Coverage can vary by date and jurisdiction, which is why often the best recourse is to contact the court itself.

H. Attorneys

Just before the opinion begins, the attorneys representing each party are listed.

I. Opinion

Finally, you reach the text of the opinion itself, beginning with the name of the authoring judge. The opinion is the portion of the case that can be cited in research. Following the majority opinion will be any concurring or dissenting opinions. A *concurrence* indicates that a judge agreed with the outcome of the case, but not the reasoning. A *special concurrence* indicates the judge agreed with both the outcome and the reasoning, but had additional comments to make. If a judge disagrees with the holding, she can author a *dissent*. Only the majority opinion is binding; however, the other opinions can nevertheless serve a research purpose as persuasive authority. Table 5-6 lists the various types of opinions.

Table 5-6. Types of Case Opinions

Type	Meaning
Majority Opinion	The opinion that the majority of judges on the court agreed with and joined.
Concurrence	Authored when a judge agrees with the outcome, but not the reasoning.
Dissent	Authored when a judge does not agree with the outcome.
Plurality	When there is no majority opinion but several concurrences; the concurring opinion with the most names attached to it is considered the plurality opinion.
Per Curiam	When no authoring judge is identified for the majority opinion; the opinion is rendered by the entire appellate panel unanimously or anonymously.
Memorandum	Typically a brief opinion, non-precedential, applying only to the parties in that case.
In Chambers	Unique to the U.S. Supreme Court, an in chambers opinion is a brief decision on a matter requiring immediacy, from the Circuit Justice to the petitioning circuit.[26]

---

26. Each Supreme Court Justice is assigned to one of the thirteen federal circuits as their Circuit Justice, for the purpose of these kinds of petitions. As of November

VI. Strategies for Reading Cases

To close out this chapter, this section provides advice on reading and analyzing cases. If you intend to rely on a case in your research, it is vital that you closely and carefully read the opinion to ensure you fully understand the outcome. This can be a painstaking task, so learning to evaluate whether a case is worth your time is an important skill to gain.

A. Selecting Cases in Research

Alluded to earlier in this chapter, two simple ways to preliminarily analyze whether a case is relevant to your research are to read through the synopsis and headnotes to a case. These will provide you a basic background, procedural posture and holding, and a list of all legal issues discussed in the opinion.

If a case passes this first inspection, start digging deeper into the opinion itself. Focus in on the parts of the opinion most germane to your research. Rarely will you find a case that is a precise match to the scenario you are researching; more likely, there are one or two legal issues that are particularly relevant. Lexis and Westlaw make it easy to jump specifically to those points in the opinion, so spend the most time there.

The first time you read the opinion, just read it. Do not try to take notes, which can become distracting and disrupt your absorption of the court's reasoning. Read first, digest, then take notes during a second reading, again focusing most closely on the legal issues nearest to your research question.

B. Analyzing a Case Opinion

Law can feel like it uses its own special language, so when you first start reading case opinions, it can be helpful to understand some basic terminology. We will use civil law cases as an example.[27] In civil litigation, the party

---

2020, Justice Amy Coney Barrett is the Circuit Justice for the Seventh Circuit. Examples of matters for which a circuit justice might be consulted are stays of execution and problems with ballot counting in an election. These matters are most often dealt with summarily, but occasionally the justice will author a short explanation, referred to as an in chambers opinion.

27. Criminal cases follow a similar pattern, with slightly different language and procedure. The rules of criminal procedure for your jurisdiction can be a helpful place to start in understanding how to read a criminal case decision.

who feels they have been wronged commences the lawsuit by filing a *complaint*. In the complaint, the filing party is referred to as the *plaintiff*, and the party the plaintiff claims to have been wronged by is the *defendant*. In the complaint, the plaintiff identifies the parties, provides the facts and the relevant laws, and asks the court for relief.[28] A full list of requirements for the complaint can be found in your jurisdiction's rules of civil procedure. The defendant then has an opportunity to respond to the complaint by filing an *answer*. In an answer, the defendant acknowledges or denies each of the facts listed in the complaint and may also raise any affirmative defenses. The time available to answer a complaint is limited by statute; if a defendant does not respond in a timely fashion, the plaintiff can request a *default judgment*, in which the court would automatically grant the plaintiff's requested relief. Throughout the life of the case, both parties and the court can submit a variety of documents that become a part of the case's docket. Following a final decision in a case, the party who lost may appeal to a higher court. The appealing party is referred to as the appellant and the other party the respondent or appellee. At the appellate level, the higher court is reviewing the lower court's decision. If they agree with the lower court, they *affirm* the decision; if they disagree, they reverse and may *remand* the case back to the lower court.

When analyzing whether a case is relevant to your research, look for factual relevance as well as legal relevance. Facts that are legally relevant are those that bear on the application or analysis of the law. These may also be referred to as material facts. Whether a fact is material depends on the case. In a case involving negligent supervision, the age of the parties might be factually significant. In a case involving an injury at a construction site, anything from lighting to signage to safety training could be factually relevant. It is rare to find a case that directly matches your legal scenario; instead, case law research is akin to assembling a jigsaw puzzle—gather a number of cases (and statutes), each of which addresses a part of your legal question, and piece these together to form your legal argument.

It should be noted that finding and addressing cases that are adverse to your legal question is just as important as finding and addressing cases that support your argument. It is unethical to ignore or avoid unfavorable cases to try to win your case. Instead, look to those negative cases and see whether you can distinguish your legal scenario from that in the adverse case.

---

28. Relief is often a request for monetary damages, but could also be injunctive relief, such as a cease-and-desist order.

Finally, once you have found an opinion you want to use in your research, there are a couple more determinative factors to consider. First, determine whether the case you are interested in has binding authority. To determine this, you have to understand the concept of *stare decisis*, the doctrine that courts have to follow prior judicial holdings on a particular legal issue in their jurisdiction. This concept takes us back to the discussion of court hierarchy at the beginning of this chapter. Within a jurisdiction, lower courts are bound by decisions of higher courts. Trial courts in Indiana are bound by the decisions of the Indiana Court of Appeals and the Indiana Supreme Court. The Indiana Court of Appeals, however, is bound by the Indiana Supreme Court, but not Indiana trial courts, because the trial courts are lower in the hierarchy. Likewise, if you are researching an issue in Indiana, and come across the perfect illustrative case from a court in Illinois, that case can only be persuasive authority, because Illinois is outside of your jurisdiction.

In applying stare decisis, courts must follow the holdings of prior cases within their hierarchy. The *holding* is the final ruling on an issue of law, and it is that language that is citable as law in a decision. Other language within the case is known as *dicta*. If the court discusses the history of a particular area of law, or postulates on how the outcome of a case would be different if particular facts were altered, this language is dicta. It can be cited as persuasive authority, but not binding precedent. Likewise, the language of a concurring or dissenting opinion can have high persuasive value, but only the language of the court's holding in the majority opinion is binding.

Once you have pieced together the legal authority that addresses your legal research question, it is important to draw on the language of the courts and the facts of each case and apply them to the facts in your own legal scenario. Mere summaries of the cases are not enough. To craft an effective legal argument, you must apply existing law to the case at hand.

Chapter 6

Case Law Research Strategies

Researching case law can be daunting. Compared to other types of legal content, the sheer volume of case law produced each year can make searching for the best cases to answer your legal research question seem a nearly impossible task. Fortunately, owing to the enormity of such a task, there are also more strategies and tools to help the researcher conduct case law research than there are for any other content type. This chapter will discuss these different approaches to case law research. Table 6-1 lists the methods for conducting case law research.

Table 6-1. Methods of Case Law Research

Method	Description
Citations in a Secondary Source	Secondary sources reference the key primary sources (statutes/cases/regulations) on topic, making this a great method to jumpstart your case law research.
Annotated Codes	The Notes Of/To Decisions in an annotated code are editorially selected cases that significantly interpret or apply the statute. When using an annotated code on Lexis or Westlaw, you also have the advantage of the citator, which provides a comprehensive list of all the cases in Lexis or Westlaw that have cited your statute.
Headnotes	The headnotes to a case in Lexis or Westlaw provide a link to all decisions that cited that case based on the legal issue identified in the headnote. This is a good method for identifying related cases.

Key Numbers or Topics	Key Numbers (Westlaw) or Topics (Lexis) are another way of identifying cases that share the same legal issue. Key Numbers and Topics are listed with the headnotes to a case, which is one way to use them to find related cases. Additionally, Westlaw offers the option to search the West Key Number System to find cases by topic.
Citing Decisions	Look to the citator report on a case (Shepard's report or tabs in Lexis, KeyCite tabs in Westlaw, BCite Analysis on Bloomberg Law) to find all cases that have cited that case. You can filter that list of citing decisions a number of ways to create a manageable research list.
Table of Authorities	Lexis, Westlaw, and Bloomberg Law likewise provide a table of authorities for each case a list of all cases cited by that case. Though these are older opinions, they can still be relevant to your research.
Keyword Searching	Like other content, you can search for relevant cases using a full-text keyword search, natural language or Boolean. You might also find the advanced search fields on Lexis and Westlaw and the Court Opinions search on Bloomberg Law particularly helpful for targeted keyword case law searches.

I. Citations in a Secondary Source

If you have consulted a secondary source in law, such as a legal encyclopedia or treatise, to ascertain background information and analysis of your legal issue, the citations in that secondary source highlight the leading primary sources, particularly case law, that address that legal issue. For this reason, one of the recommended strategies for conducting legal research, as discussed in Chapter 10, is to start with secondary sources. For example, if you had a client in a small, rural community in Indiana who was having a dispute with his neighbor over the fence that divides their properties, you might first consult the *Indiana Law Encyclopedia* for entries pertaining to fence law. Your research leads you to an entry in the encyclopedia on spite fences.[1] As you read this entry and learn about the nuisance cause of action for building a spite fence, you notice that the footnotes reference two Indiana

---

1. Laura Hunter Dietz, Spite Fences as Nuisance, 1 *Ind. Law Encyc.* § 18 (current through Feb. 2022).

statutes[2] and two Indiana cases, *Gertz v. Estes*[3] and *Wernke v. Halas*.[4] As your research continues, these will be two helpful cases to jumpstart your case law research.

II. Annotated Codes

If your research has led you to a relevant statute pertaining to your legal issue, the case annotations in an annotated statutory code can provide an additional source of potentially relevant case law. Recall from Chapter 4 that case annotations are editorially selected cases that significantly analyze, interpret, and apply that particular statute. While these are not a comprehensive list of all cases that have cited the statute, nor are all of the case annotations necessarily germane to your particular research question, this list of cases is nevertheless a helpful place to start when transitioning from statutory to case law research.

Continuing with the example from the previous section, if you expanded your research on spite fence law by first exploring the statutes cited in the encyclopedia entry, you might look at the case annotations from Indiana Code § 32-26-10-1 to look for relevant Indiana cases. You find that, in addition to the *Gertz* and *Wernke* cases highlighted by the encyclopedia, the case annotations to the statute also refer you to *Giller v. West*[5] and *Grooms v. Meriweather*.[6] It is worth recalling here that case annotations are referred to as Notes of Decisions in Westlaw and in annotated codes published by Thomson West, and Notes to Decisions in Lexis and in annotated codes published by LexisNexis. Remember also that, because these are editorially selected cases, and there are different editorial teams at West and Lexis, the cases highlighted in the case annotations to the same statute can vary; for instance, Westlaw's case annotations reference *Gertz*, *Wernke*, *Giller*, and *Grooms*, but Lexis' case annotations reference only *Gertz* and *Grooms*. If you have the advantage of access to both services, therefore, it can be best practice to examine both, to make sure you are not missing additional relevant cases.

---

2. Ind. Code § 32-26-10-1 and Ind. Code § 32-26-10-2.
3. 879 N.E.2d 617 (Ind. Ct. App. 2008).
4. 600 N.E.2d 117 (Ind. Ct. App. 1992).
5. 69 N.E. 548 (Ind. 1904).
6. 137 N.E. 32 (Ind. Ct. App. 1922).

III. Headnotes & Key Numbers

Owing to the vastness of the body of case law, one thing that sets case law apart from researching other types of law are the specialized tools that have been created specifically for case law research. These tools have historic origins, developed in the 1800s, when the volume of case law was first starting to multiply. At that time, commercial reporters, as discussed in Chapter 5, were making case opinions more accessible to attorneys, but, because reporters are published chronologically, case law research was still a challenge. There was no effective means of researching cases by subject. The West Publishing Company, the predominant publisher of case reporters at the time, sought to solve this problem, and in so doing, created two related tools researchers still use today to locate cases by topic: headnotes and key numbers.

A. West Key Number System

To begin this task, the editorial team at the West Publishing Company generated a list of all topics in American law, starting with the broadest topics, such as criminal law and tort law. They then broke these topics down into smaller and smaller topics; for example, within criminal law, they could distinguish between crimes to property and crimes to the person, and within a particular crime, they could include topics on each element of the crime and all defenses. This resulted in a vast topic tree of all legal issues in American law.[7] After organizing this system of topics, they assigned each topic a number, and referred to them as *key numbers*.[8]

B. Headnotes

Next, as they prepared to publish the text of case opinions in their reporters, the editorial team would scour each opinion, identify every individual issue of law in the case, and summarize it. They would then look to the West Key Number System to determine what topic and subtopic best fit that particular legal issue.[9] When printing the case opinion in the West reporter, each

---

7. The West editorial team continues to expand and develop this topic tree to this day, to reflect the ever-changing nature of law.

8. In print reporters and digests, you will see a key icon within each key number.

9. You will often see a headnote to a case that has been assigned more than one key number. This simply means that the legal issue summarized in that headnote can

case would start with a list of these legal issue summaries, called *headnotes*, because they are printed at the beginning (head) of the case; the corresponding key number was printed above the text of the headnote.

C. Digests

With the creation of headnotes and key numbers, the West Publishing Company was half-way toward their goal of providing a means to locate cases by topic; however, adding headnotes and key numbers to a reporter alone did not solve the problem—cases in reporters are still published chronologically. What they needed was a separate publication, coordinated with the reporters, that would serve as an aid to finding relevant cases in the print reporters. Therefore, the West Publishing Company created a publication called a *digest*, organized by the West Key Number System. The volumes of a digest are arranged alphabetically by topic, and following each key number are published the headnotes to cases that fall under that key number. To find cases by subject, an attorney would go to the print digest, locate the topic and key number he sought to research, and read the text of the headnotes that were listed under that key number. If he found a headnote that interested him, the headnote would include a citation to the reporter where the full text of the opinion was published, and the attorney would then use that citation to locate the full-text opinion of the case in the reporter.

The West Publishing Company created digests for federal cases and every state; thus, if you were conducting Indiana case law research and needed to find a case on a particular topic, you would browse the *Indiana Digest*, find a relevant topic and key number, and see what headnotes to Indiana cases were printed below that key number. You would then use the case citation listed in the digest to find the full text of the case in the relevant reporter. The beauty of the West Key Number System is its uniformity. If there are no headnotes printed under a particular key number in the *Indiana Digest*, indicating that this is a legal issue that has not yet been dealt with by Indiana courts, you could go to the *Illinois* or *Ohio Digest*, look under the same key number, and look for headnotes to cases from those jurisdictions to use as persuasive authority.

---

fit into more than one legal topic in the key number system. In this way, headnotes are narrower than key numbers.

D. Headnotes, Key Numbers, and Digests in an Online Environment

Thomson West continues to publish digests in print to this day, but with the advent of online legal research systems, you can also use these tools when conducting electronic legal research. The West Key Number System is incorporated into the Westlaw database. Just as in a print reporter, if you look up a case in Westlaw, you will find headnotes published at the beginning of the case, with relevant key numbers published along with each headnote. If you click on the key number, you are taken to a digest page in Westlaw that lists all the headnotes to cases in that jurisdiction that fall under that key number (you can expand or contract the jurisdiction as well). In addition, following the text of each headnote in the case, you will see a link that says "# Cases that Cite This Headnote." If clicked, this takes you to a narrowed list of citing decisions that cited to that particular case based on the legal issue summarized in that headnote. This is an excellent way to find related cases; if you look through the headnotes to a case and find one or two that pertain to the legal issue you are most interested in researching, the cases that cite that headnote share the same legal issue in common.

While the West Key Number System is proprietary to Thomson Reuters, Lexis has developed its own topic and headnote system as well. When reading cases on Lexis, you will find LexisNexis Headnotes at the beginning of each case that pull out the individual issues of law in the case, providing direct quotes from the opinion where those legal issues are discussed. Above each headnote, you will find corresponding topics, which function very similarly to West Key Numbers. Clicking on a topic takes you to a topic document, where you will find a listing of all documents in Lexis (not just cases) that the Lexis editorial team has classified under that topic; you can narrow down that list to cases, to find all cases in Lexis that fall under that topic, and narrow further still to cases within a particular jurisdiction. Additionally, following the text of the headnote in Lexis, you will find a link that says "Shepardize—Narrow by this headnote." Similar to Westlaw, this link will take you to an abbreviated list of citing decisions that cite to that particular case based on the issue of law in that headnote.[10]

---

10. Bloomberg Law has developed a tool similar to headnotes, Points of Law, that will highlight passages within a case and provide a list of cases that have cited the instant case based on the issue (point of law) covered in that highlighted passage.

IV. Citators

Citators serve a number of functions and will be discussed more fully in Chapter 7; but they are worth noting here for two additional ways to find cases.

A. Citing References

When you pull up a case in Lexis, Westlaw, or Bloomberg Law and examine the citator information, the citator identifies every document on that particular legal research platform that cites to that case. This includes not only other cases that have cited that case, but also documents such as secondary sources. *Citing decisions* are a subset of this group of citing references and refer specifically to all cases that have cited the featured case.[11] This list is comprehensive, and if you are looking at a landmark case, the list of citing decisions could include thousands of cases, but the citator provides a number of ways to filter the list to a more manageable and relevant number. These options will be discussed in detail in Chapter 7.

B. Table of Authorities

Citators on Lexis, Westlaw, and Bloomberg Law today also provide a Table of Authorities for each case. While citing decisions are later cases that have cited to the featured case, the table of authorities lists *cited decisions*—all the cases that the featured case cites to. The researcher's inclination may be to focus on the most recent cases, as being most indicative of the court's current reasoning, but the table of authorities can still be a powerful tool. The cited decisions may very well include landmark cases on a particular topic, and as such, their precedential value should not be overlooked.

V. Full-Text Searching

While case law research on Lexis, Westlaw, and Bloomberg Law includes several specialized tools for researching cases specifically, full-text searching is still among the first steps most researchers will take in a database when beginning the research process.

---

11. Bloomberg Law's citing decisions are referred to as Case Analysis and other citing references are referred to as Citing Documents; both are found by clicking on the "BCite Analysis" link to the right of a case opinion.

A. Natural Language

Natural language searching has already been discussed in Chapter 2, but as the most common method of full-text searching today, it bears repeating. A natural language search is what we commonly think of as "googling"—typing a few keywords or a phrase into the search box and hitting search. Quick, but not necessarily efficient. While the search engines on modern databases like Lexis and Westlaw are designed to support natural language searching, a natural language search most often yields a high volume of search results, many of which are irrelevant. You can often salvage a high-yield natural language search by taking advantage of the search result filters the database provides. Table 6-2 highlights several helpful filters.

Table 6-2. Search Filters on Lexis and Westlaw

Type of Filter	Purpose
Content Type/ Category	Filter a general search to a particular type of legal content, such as Cases, Statutes, or Secondary Sources.
Court/Jurisdiction	If you are researching Indiana cases, you could filter to Indiana. Lexis, Westlaw, and Bloomberg Law separate federal and state jurisdictions as well; if your legal issue could have a federal component, you may want to filter to both Federal > 7th Circuit and State > Indiana, to capture both state and federal cases in Indiana's jurisdiction.
Topic/Key Number	You can take advantage of the topic and key number systems on Lexis and Westlaw by filtering to recommended topics. In Westlaw search results, this is the Key Number filter; in Lexis, it is the Practice Area & Topics filter. Bloomberg Law has a topic filter as well, though it is broader than either Lexis or Westlaw's.
Search Within Results	Another simple way to refine a keyword search is to filter further by an additional keyword. Both Lexis and Westlaw include a small "search within results" search bar to the left of the search results list where you can add these additional search terms.

B. Terms & Connectors

You can strengthen your full-text keyword searches by learning a few simple terms and connectors. These connectors empower you to take more control over your search by instructing the search algorithm to treat your keywords in a particular way. Table 6-3 highlights a few simple, yet effective terms and connectors.[12]

Table 6-3. Terms & Connectors

Term/Connector	Purpose	Example
Double quotation marks ""	Treat terms as a phrase	"spite fence"
AND or &	Retrieve only results containing both/all search terms	spite & fence spite and fence and nuisance
OR	Retrieve results containing either term—helpful if there are synonyms for your keyword	(spite or nuisance)[13] and fence
NOT, AND NOT, %	Retrieve results containing one term, but not another—helpful if you are researching a topic commonly searched in conjunction with another	fence not spite (This will retrieve case law involving fences, but not spite fences.)
!	Root expander—helps you search multiple variations of a word	fenc! (would yield fence, fenced, fences, fencing, fencer, etc.)
*	Wildcard—helps you search a term that has multiple spellings	mari*uana (yields results with marijuana or marihuana)

---

12. For a full list of terms and connectors available on Lexis and Westlaw, refer to their advanced search pages. To get to this page, click the Advanced link to the right of the main search bar. To see available terms and connectors for Bloomberg Law, click on the question mark icon to the right of the search bar.

13. While spite and nuisance are not true synonyms, in the legal world, some jurisdictions refer to spite fences, and others refer to nuisance fences, so this will get to either—cases involving the construction of fences to annoy a neighbor. It should also be noted that the parentheses here allow you to group terms in your search. Algorithms are mathematical in their analysis of a search phrase, so the search algorithm here will know to first process the spite and nuisance terms, then the fence term.

C. Advanced Search

A third means of conducting a full-text keyword search for cases is to make use of the advanced search pages on Lexis, Westlaw, and Bloomberg Law. If you are unsure of how to construct a terms-and-connectors search, the advanced search pages on Lexis and Westlaw start by offering those specialized search fields. This is the type of advanced search feature you have likely seen on other databases (e.g., a search bar that says "Include all of these terms" or "This exact phrase"). What makes these pages more useful for legal research, particularly case law, are the document-specific search fields that allow you to search for your keywords in particular parts of the document, rather than anywhere in the document. You may also see this referred to as *field* or *segment* searching. Case law has the most available fields of any content type in Lexis or Westlaw.

There is one critical wrinkle in advanced searching on Lexis and Westlaw: Getting to the correct advanced search page. The advanced search link features prominently to the right of the main search bar on both Lexis and Westlaw. However, if you are on the home page of either database and you click this link, the advanced search page you see is nothing special; it features the basic Boolean search bars, but the "unique" document fields are (1) title, (2) citation, and (3) date. Because you have not yet filtered to any particular content type, this advanced search page displays the fields common to every type of document in Lexis or Westlaw —most everything has a title, citation, and date. You will need to filter by content type to see the truly unique search fields available on Lexis and Westlaw. Lexis makes this easy. From the top of the advanced search page, next to "Search Everything," you can select a specific content type, like cases. On Westlaw, it takes a couple more steps. Back on the home page, below the search bar, navigate to the "Cases" page. Select the same link for advanced search at the top of the page, and you will be brought to the "Advanced: Cases" search page. Scrolling down, you will see all the unique case law search fields available. Most of these fields overlap on Lexis and Westlaw. Table 6-4 highlights several helpful fields on each platform.[14]

___

14. For advanced searching of cases on Bloomberg Law, you can use its separate Court Opinions Search link from the Bloomberg Law homepage. It does not offer as many specialized fields as Lexis or Westlaw, but you can pre-filter by court, topic, party, case name, judge, or attorney/firm.

Table 6-4. Advanced Search Fields for Case Law Research

Field	Purpose	Lexis	Westlaw
Party Name	If you are searching for a case and you only know the name of one of the parties. This can be helpful if you have read about a case in the news, because most news coverage will not provide case citation information.	✓	✓
Synopsis	Brief description of the case, including procedural posture and holding, that appears before the text of the opinion; most often written by the editorial team of the reporter, rather than the court	✓ (Called Summary)	✓
Headnote	Looks for your search term in the text of the headnotes to a case	✓	✓ (In Westlaw, you can also use the Digest field to search your keyword in both the headnote and key number text.)
Words & Phrases	A unique tool, part of the print digest system, this field allows you to search for cases that have judicially defined your keyword.	X (This tool is unique to Westlaw.)	✓

Depending on your research goals, there are many other case law search fields you might want to explore. For instance, if you are looking for an opinion written by a particular judge, there are several fields that may be of use, including individual fields for Concurrences and Dissents. When looking at the available fields in Lexis or Westlaw, if you are uncertain what a particular field will search, both Lexis and Westlaw offer an annotated case with all fields labeled. This helpful document is available on the right of the advanced search page.

Chapter 7

Citators

It is your ethical duty as an attorney to be a competent researcher. Part of this competence comes from finding the most relevant legal authority for your case; but another significant part involves ensuring that the authority you cite is good law. The primary tool attorneys use to ensure this is a *citator*.

One of the earliest citators for American case law was *Shepard's Adhesive Annotations*, first published in the late 1800s as a print subscription service that allowed attorneys to track the case treatment of new and existing case law. The service grew and evolved over the years, purchased by LexisNexis in the 1990s. The Lexis citator is still called Shepard's today. As Westlaw developed its own online platform, they developed their own citator, KeyCite, that functions similarly to Shepard's. Bloomberg Law, too, has developed its own citator, BCite.

As citators evolved, particularly in an electronic environment, they grew to serve additional purposes. This chapter will discuss the many uses of a citator in legal research. Citator information on both Lexis and Westlaw is divided among tabs across the top of the document, reflecting the different types of information the citator provides.[1] On Bloomberg Law, the citator report, only available for cases, is found by clicking on the BCite Analysis link to the right of the case opinion.

---

1. On Lexis, you can also get to the citator report by clicking the "Shepardize document" link to the right of the document.

I. Updating Cases

The original and arguably still most important use of a citator is to check the *treatment status* of any case you intend to rely on in your research. A case's treatment status includes whether the case has been positively or negatively cited by other courts or whether overturned in whole or in part. This is crucial information to have when conducting legal research, because you do not want to rely on a case that is no longer good law.

The treatment status of a case is most easily discernible from the treatment symbol attributed to it by the citator. These colorful symbols indicate a case's treatment status. Every major legal research citator uses a similar color scheme for their treatment indicators. If a case has a red symbol, it means some or all of the case has been overturned. If a case has a yellow symbol, the case has received some criticism, but still remains good law. If a case has overall positive treatment by later cases, the case will have either a green symbol, or no symbol at all. Table 7-1 provides a description of the types of symbols found via Shepard's, KeyCite, and BCite.

Table 7-1. Treatment symbols in Shepard's, KeyCite, and BCite

Symbol Color	Meaning	Lexis/ Shepard's	Westlaw/ KeyCite	Bloomberg Law/ BCite
Red	Most negative treatment; some or all of the case has been overruled or reversed	✓	✓	✓
Orange	The validity of the case has been called into question; overruling risk	✓	✓	✓ (In Bloomberg Law, this color indicates a case has been superseded or rendered obsolete by an intervening statute or regulation.)

Yellow	Lesser negative treatment; a case may criticize or distinguish itself from the court's holding.	✓	✓	✓ (Yellow on Bloomberg Law means criticism of the legal reasoning of the case by later courts or modification of a case holding within the case's direct history.)
Green	Positive treatment	✓	X (In Westlaw, positive treatment is indicated by a lack of a treatment symbol.)	✓
Blue	Neutral treatment	✓	X	✓ (Blue on Bloomberg Law indicates a later case differentiates this opinion from the later case's holding.)
Blue-and-white	Appeal pending	X	✓	X

A quick look at the treatment symbol alone is not sufficient to analyze a case's current treatment status. In fact, on occasion, the same case pulled up on Lexis, Westlaw, and Bloomberg Law will have a different treatment symbol on each service, so interpretation and application of these symbols can vary. Rather, these are quick visual guides to provide a general idea. When analyzing a case with a red symbol, for example, it is important to look at the case more closely to determine what aspect of the case has been overruled or reversed. If the legal issue you are most interested in is not the legal issue whose holding was overruled or reversed, that element of the case's holding is still good law for your research purposes. As the researcher, the ultimate analysis of any resource ends with you.

II. Expanding Your Case Law Research

As mentioned in Chapter 6, another important use of a citator is to find other related cases. The citator provides this list in two forms: citing decisions and the table of authorities.

A. Citing Decisions

The list of citing decisions is a comprehensive list of all cases that have cited to the featured case.[2] Depending on the case, this list can be extremely long, even thousands of cases, especially when viewing a landmark federal decision. In fact, this can be a good indication of the strength of a particular case—the greater number of citing decisions, the stronger the precedent. If you are looking for additional cases, and you have found one case that is particularly relevant, this list of citing decisions can be a solid strategy for finding additional cases to support your research. However, it would be unreasonable to imagine that you would read every case listed in the citing decisions; indeed, it is likely that the majority are irrelevant to your particular research quest. The citators on Lexis, Westlaw, and Bloomberg Law provide similar filters for narrowing and refining this list of citing decisions to a more relevant and manageable list, as described in Table 7-2.

---

2. All cases within the Lexis, Westlaw, or Bloomberg Law platform. It is not unusual for the number of citing decisions for a case to vary when viewed in Lexis, Westlaw, and Bloomberg Law. This most commonly can be attributed to a difference in the number of unreported decisions on each platform.

Table 7-2. Citing Decision Filters

Filter	Purpose	Lexis/ Shepard's	Westlaw/ KeyCite	Bloomberg Law/BCite
Analysis/Treatment	How does the citing decision treat the featured case?	✓ (several options, corresponding to the array of treatment symbols— positive, negative, questioning, neutral)	✓ (focuses on negative treatment)	✓
Depth of Discussion	How much does the citing decision discuss the featured case? Indicated graphically in all three services by 0–4 (or 5) bars.	✓	✓	✓
Headnotes	How many legal issues does the citing decision have in common with the featured case?[3]	✓	✓	X
Jurisdiction/Court	Narrow citing decisions by state and federal jurisdiction	✓	✓	✓

---

3. This can be a good tool to use to narrow the citing decisions. If you have already analyzed the list of legal issues for the featured case, and determined which headnote(s) is most relevant to your research question, narrowing the citing decisions by those headnotes can help you find the most similar cases.

| Reported/Publica-tion Status | Optionally, filter out unreported decisions[4] | ✓ | ✓ | X |
| Search Within Results | Perform a full-text keyword search of the citing decisions | ✓ | ✓ | X |

B. Table of Authorities (Cited Decisions)

Citators today also include a Table of Authorities for a case, providing a list of all cases that are cited by a case (cited decisions). These are older opinions, but can nevertheless be helpful to a researcher—if the older case is still good law, it is still a valuable research source. The tables of authorities provided by both Shepard's and KeyCite have fewer filtering options than the citing decisions list. Both allow you to search within results. Shepard's additionally allows you to filter by analysis or jurisdiction. BCite offers the same filters for Tables of Authorities as for Citing Decisions.

C. Other Citing Sources

Citators have expanded to include not only comprehensive lists of citing decisions for a case, but also a comprehensive list of all other documents that have cited the case. This includes primarily secondary sources, such as law review articles or treatises, but also court documents, such as briefs. Shepard's on Lexis provides fewer filters for Other Citing Sources, limited primarily to searching within results or restricting by date. Westlaw's KeyCite is slightly more expansive, allowing you to filter by headnote as well. Bloomberg Law's BCite Citing Documents allows you to filter by content type, date, or practice area.

---

4. This is helpful if you are in a jurisdiction that does not allow you to cite unreported cases.

III. Case History

The citator also provides access to the history of the case, helpful for accessing the lower (or higher) court opinion, and court filings, if available.

IV. Beyond Case Law

A final important note about citators today is that they have expanded beyond case law to be a tool for statutory, regulatory, and even secondary source research as well. If you are researching a legal problem and find a statute that is relevant to your research but want to expand further and find cases related to the statute, the citator in Lexis or Westlaw will provide citing decisions and other citing references for that statute, just as they will for a case.[5] This makes it very easy to transition from statutory to case law research.

---

5. While Bloomberg Law's citator is restricted to cases, it has developed a separate tool, Smart Code®, for regulatory and statutory research that will identify cases that have cited a regulation or statute.

Chapter 8

Administrative Law Research

Administrative law research covers a wide array of documents, from regulations to administrative decisions, attorney general opinions to executive orders. Not all legal questions involve administrative law, but highly regulated industries, such as tax, health law, environmental law, and securities, do. It is always a good idea to ask yourself whether administrative law might come into play in your legal research question. If so, finding the appropriate regulations, decisions, and guidance documents will be critical to seeking out a complete answer.

Administrative law, broadly, refers to the law produced by the executive branch, including the president (at the federal level), the governor (at the state level), and federal and state administrative agencies. Just like the legislature and the courts, these entities can produce documents that have the force of law, as well as a number of other types of documents that provide interpretation and explanation of these laws. This chapter will focus primarily on the work of agencies, concluding with a section on presidential and gubernatorial documents.

I. The Legal Authority of Agencies

Agencies derive their powers from statutory authority; therefore, in order to determine the powers of an agency, refer to your jurisdiction's statutory code. The foundation of administrative law in any jurisdiction will be found in its *administrative procedure act*. This law dictates the administrative process in a particular jurisdiction, as well as the powers bestowed on that jurisdiction's agencies. The Indiana Administrative Procedures Act can be found in Indiana Code title 4, article 22. The statutes in this article spell out which agencies are governed by this article and which are excluded,[1] the rulemaking process in Indiana, and other procedural specifics.

A jurisdiction's administrative procedure act can imbue an agency with two different types of powers: quasi-legislative and quasi-judicial. Agencies with the power to create *regulations* (also referred to as *rules*) are said to have a *quasi-legislative* function, because regulations operate similarly to statutes. When disputes arise over agency regulations, agencies may be empowered to conduct administrative hearings, similar to judicial proceedings, to settle the administrative dispute; this is referred to as a *quasi-judicial* power.

II. Administrative Regulations

The power to create administrative regulations is considered a quasi-legislative function of an administrative agency; but the process of creating an administrative regulation is far different than the legislative process of enacting a bill into law.

A. Enabling Acts

Agencies cannot act without express authority from the legislature; therefore, you can look for a statute called an *enabling act* that directs a specific agency to create regulations on a specific topic.[2] As an example, think of endangered species. Before we had laws on this topic, legislators conferred with constituents and decided it was important for us to protect endangered species. They passed a law, the Endangered Species Act, that established this intent. Within that act, Congress directs the head of the U.S. Fish & Wildlife Service to create regulations to move the endangered species program forward. By so doing, they enabled the agency to act. Within the bounds of the statutory language of that enabling act, the U.S. Fish & Wildlife Service was

---

1. Ind. Code § 4-22-2-3: "'Agency' means any officer, board, commission, department, division, bureau, committee, or other governmental entity exercising any of the executive (including the administrative) powers of state government. The term does not include the judicial or legislative departments of state government or a political subdivision...."

2. This can be a very broad delegation of authority, covering a sweeping subject, like tax law, but it can also be a more specific delegation of authority, pertaining to a narrower topic within that broader legal arena, such as the authority to create regulations that support a particular new tax statute. Enabling authority may also come from the president or governor through an executive order.

empowered to promulgate regulations on the subject of protecting endangered species.

Often litigation against an agency revolves around questions of whether the agency overstepped its bounds when creating particular regulations; when such litigation occurs, the court will refer back to the statutory authority to see what scope was intended for that agency to act within. It is therefore important when conducting administrative law research to also look to this enabling authority to fully understand the intended scope behind an agency's actions.

B. The Rulemaking Process

The process of creating a regulation is also vastly different from the legislative process. As seen in Table 8-1, the general process of promulgating a regulation requires an agency to publish the text of a proposed rule and allow a brief window, known as the *notice and comment period*, for the public to submit feedback on the proposed language; the agency then considers the public comments before publishing the finalized version of the regulation.

Table 8-1. Basic Rulemaking Process

Each jurisdiction's process will vary slightly, and there can be exceptions (e.g., in the case of emergency or temporary regulations), but this is the general flow. The administrative procedure act will detail the specifics of your jurisdiction's regulatory process. In Indiana, an agency first provides notice of an intent to adopt a new rule,[3] which triggers the notice and comment period,[4] after which the agency considers and responds to these comments,[5] before drafting the final text of the rule. This is then sent to the Indiana Attorney General[6] and Governor for approval,[7] before the finalized text is

---

3. Ind. Code § 4-22-2-23.
4. Ind. Code § 4-22-2-23.1.
5. *Id.* at subsection (e).
6. Ind. Code § 4-22-2-31, § 4-22-2-32.
7. Ind. Code § 4-22-2-33, § 4-22-2-34.

published. In this way, regulations are radically different sources of law than statutes, because the public has the chance to weigh in on how the regulation should be drafted before it takes effect.

To learn more about the rulemaking process in Indiana, you may want to consult the *Administrative Rules Drafting Manual*, available from the Indiana General Assembly website under "Publications."[8] Although written for those who draft Indiana regulations, the information contained in this manual provides insight beneficial to anyone interested in the rulemaking process in Indiana, from when and where to submit the proposed and final text of rules, down to the components of a printed rule itself.

C. Researching Indiana Regulations

Indiana regulations are published in two different publications. Proposed and final regulations are published in the *Indiana Register*. This is a chronological publication of regulations. It began publication in 1978 as a monthly print publication. It ceased print publication in 2006 and is now electronic-only,[9] published on a more frequent basis. The *Indiana Register* contains all rules submitted to the Indiana Secretary of State, as well as proposed rules, emergency rules, and other documents, such as official opinions of the state attorney general and executive orders of the governor. If you wanted to conduct a regulatory history on an Indiana regulation, to see how its language has changed from the proposed to finalized text, you would refer to the *Indiana Register*.

As a chronological publication, the *Indiana Register* is not the strongest research tool, which is why the Indiana General Assembly called for a codification of Indiana regulations, organizing them by subject. Once a finalized regulation has been published in the *Indiana Register*, therefore, it gets codified and published a second time, in the *Indiana Administrative Code*. The *Indiana Administrative Code* began publication in 1979. From 1979 to 2003, the *Indiana Administrative Code* underwent a series of recompilations every 3–5 years, in 1984, 1988, 1992, 1996, 2001, and 2003. Between recompilation years, the Code would be updated annually with a cumulative supplement. Since 2003, the Code has been recompiled every year. It is the official publication of Indiana's regulations and the only place today to find all of Indiana's

---

8. Available at http://iac.iga.in.gov/iac/IACDrftMan.pdf.

9. *Indiana Register* available at http://iac.iga.in.gov/iac/irtoc.htm.

published regulations.[10] While the *Indiana Register* contains both proposed and final rules, the *Indiana Administrative Code* contains the text of final rules only, in codified form. Until recently, the *Indiana Administrative Code* was published in print as well as electronically; as of 2020, the print publication has ceased. The official, authenticated version can be found on the Indiana General Assembly's website.[11] If you are citing to a final regulation, when possible, cite to the *Indiana Administrative Code*. Table 8-2 describes the coverage of the *Indiana Register* and the *Indiana Administrative Code* on the state government website, Lexis, and Westlaw.[12]

Table 8-2. Indiana Regulations on IN.gov, Lexis, and Westlaw

	IN.gov	Lexis	Westlaw
Indiana Register	Oct. 2000–present	Current and archive back to 1998	Selected coverage; current and archive back to 2000
Indiana Administrative Code	2003–present	Current and archive back to 2010	Current and archive back to 2002

D. Researching Regulations on IN.gov

The current *Indiana Register* and *Indiana Administrative Code* can be accessed for free on the Indiana General Assembly website, under "Publications," and on commercial databases. As shown in Table 8-2, the website also contains an archive of these publications, with the *Indiana Register* back to October 2000 and the *Indiana Administrative Code* back to 2003. You can browse either publication, or search by citation or keyword.

For example, if you had a small chicken coop in your backyard and wanted to start selling chicken eggs at your local farmer's market, you would

---

10. Throughout the state's history, there have been various private and commercial compilations of Indiana regulations, but none remain in publication today. For more information about the history of the publication of Indiana regulations, consult the introduction to the *User's Guide to the -IR- Database*, available at http://iac.iga.in.gov/iac//faqs.pdf.

11. 2003 to current, http://iac.iga.in.gov/iac//iacarchive.htm.

12. The current version of the *Indiana Administrative Code* is also available on Bloomberg Law. A short archive of material from the *Indiana Register* is searchable as well, under the category "Indiana Rulemaking."

need to know what regulations exist regarding the packaging of chicken eggs. Since you would be looking for a current regulation, you might search the latest update to the *Indiana Administrative Code* only; and an initial search in the IR Database on the Indiana General Assembly website for "egg container" returns seven results. The first result looks most promising, a regulation from Title 370, Article 1, regulations of the Indiana Egg Board. One quirk of the IR Database to be aware of is that, to view the authenticated PDF of the regulation, the link opens a PDF of the entire article, not just the individual section; you will need to search the PDF again to find your specific regulation.[13] Here, you will find "370 IAC 1-3-3.1 Consumer packages; packaging materials," which states that, if selling eggs in a retail establishment, the eggs must be packaged in new containers, but an exception is made for farmers markets, where containers can be reused.[14] Alternatively, if you knew the citation to your Indiana regulation already, you could enter the title and article numbers[15] in the IAC Cite box and pull up the PDF directly.

E. Researching Indiana Regulations on Westlaw

To search Indiana regulations on Westlaw, from the home page, click on "State," choose Indiana, and click on "Indiana Regulations." This brings up the *Indiana Administrative Code*. You can browse the titles or search with the search bar at the top of the page. An advantage to searching Indiana regulations on Westlaw is access to citator information for the codified regulation. If you pull up a regulation from the *Indiana Administrative Code* on Westlaw, you will have access to any available case annotations (Notes of Decisions), history notes, and citing references. For the example in the previous section, 370 IAC 1-3-3.1 has no citing references, but does have ten history documents, helpful if you want to research the history of this regulation.

---

13. To search the PDF, click Ctrl+F or Command+F and use the search box that pops up to search the document by keyword.

14. 370 IAC 1-3-3.1, http://www.in.gov/legislative/iac/pdf-iac/iac2006oldfmt/T03700/A00010.PDF?IACT=370.

15. In this example, the title is 370 and the article is 1.

The *Indiana Register* is less obvious on Westlaw. From the same location where you found the *Indiana Administrative Code*, look to the right under the "Tools & Resources" menu, and you will see "Indiana Proposed & Adopted Regulations—Current." This link takes you to the most recent two years of proposed and finalized regulations from Indiana state agencies. From this page, the "Tools & Resources" menu allows you to access two additional historical Indiana regulatory collections. "Indiana Proposed & Adopted Regulations-All" provides access to all proposed and finalized regulations from Indiana state agencies from 2006 to present. "Indiana Administrative Register-Historical" provides access to issues of the *Indiana Register* from October 2000 to December 19, 2013. You cannot browse the *Indiana Register*, only search. Citator information is not available for the *Indiana Register*.

F. Researching Indiana Regulations on Lexis

If you pull up the Indiana collection from the home page on Lexis, under "Administrative Materials, Codes, and Regulations," you have separate links for the *Indiana Register* and the *Indiana Administrative Code*. Lexis does not provide access to citator information for the *Indiana Administrative Code*, but you can compare versions, to see what changes have been made to the regulatory language over time. For the egg carton example, you can compare the regulation every year since 2018.

You can search the *Indiana Register* back to 1998 on Lexis, choosing to search all years or a specific year. Once again, citator information is unavailable.

G. Researching Indiana Regulations on Bloomberg Law

To get to Indiana regulations on Bloomberg Law, from the Browse menu, click on "Laws & Regulations," then "State Laws & Regulations," and click on Indiana from the interactive map. You can browse the current *Indiana Administrative Code* by clicking the gray T.O.C. button to the right of the heading. Alternatively, you can search either (or both) the *Indiana Administrative Code* or the *Indiana Register* (listed as Indiana Rulemaking) by checking the box next to the heading and crafting your search in the search box at the top of the page. Bloomberg Law's Smart Code® tool is available for state regulatory research, to help you find any citing decisions.

III. Agency Decisions

Recall that the administrative procedure act can imbue an agency with both a quasi-legislative power, the ability to promulgate regulations, and a quasi-judicial power, the ability to settle disputes over their regulations and regulatory programs. In Indiana, some state agencies have statutorily established adjudicatory bodies, but for those that do not, Indiana Code § 4-15-10.5 provides for their adjudicatory procedure. Under this chapter, the Office of Administrative Law Proceedings may provide the agency with an independent administrative law judge to preside over agency disputes and render verdicts. Indiana Code § 4-21.5 then provides detail on administrative notices and adjudicative proceedings. There is no official publication for agency adjudications, but agencies are required to index any final orders from an adjudication and make them available for public inspection upon request.[16] The agency must also maintain an official record of the proceeding, including documents compiled during the proceeding, prior to the issuance of the final order.[17] Agency administrative decisions are typically non-precedential, but binding on the immediate parties involved, and can be highly persuasive in later administrative disputes.

A. Researching Agency Decisions on IN.gov

Because there is no official publication for agency decisions, it is up to the individual agency whether it will make its decisions available on its website. For example, the Indiana Office of Environmental Adjudication offers a "Decisions Database" on its website, with all Final Orders available from 1999 forward.[18] You can browse the decisions by year, and they also offer a simple search box; the search results that come up are not uniformly named,[19] so navigating the results can be a challenge, but at the bottom of the page, the database recommends related searches. For example, if you were looking for decisions pertaining to environmental issues surrounding coal, a simple

---

16. Ind. Code § 4-21.5-3-32.

17. Ind. Code § 4-21.5-3-33. Subsection (b) of this statute lays out a list of 11 documents that go into this record.

18. All final orders are available from 1999 on: https://www.in.gov/oea/decisions/.

19. A search for "coal" returns results with a URL as the header or a citation as the header; occasionally the result snippets provide party names, but not always.

search for "coal" yields 28 results, but the database recommends other, narrower searches, such as "coal company" or "coal mine."

B. Agency Decisions on Westlaw

In the Indiana collection on Westlaw, under "Administrative Decisions & Guidance," you can access agency materials for seven categories of Indiana agencies and the Indiana Attorney General. Indiana Environmental Decisions includes the Office of Environmental Adjudication, the Indiana Air Pollution Control Board, and the Indiana Department of Environmental Management, with decisions from 1989 forward. While search results here are clearer and easier to read than on the agency's own database, there are no advanced editorial features for Indiana agency decisions on Westlaw (such as citator information)—just the text of the decision itself.

C. Agency Decisions on Lexis

In the Indiana collection on Lexis, under "Administrative Materials, Codes, and Regulations," Lexis provides administrative decisions and other agency materials from ten agencies and the Indiana Attorney General. A search of the Indiana Office of Environmental Adjudication here takes you to an advanced search screen; you can search decisions back to 1997, and while the search results are clearer and easier to read here than on the agency's website, Lexis provides only the text of the decision, with no editorial enhancements.

D. Other Agency Documents

In addition to administrative decisions and regulations, agencies produce a plethora of other documents intended to help explain and interpret their regulatory agenda. These documents vary by agency; some agencies are required to submit annual or event-triggered reports to the Indiana General Assembly;[20] some may issue advisory letters; others may publish newsletters, pamphlets, and other guidance documents for public benefit. While non-precedential, these documents can be highly persuasive in hearings or litigation involving the state agency. The best means for finding agency publications is from the agency's website.[21]

---

20. These reports are available on the Indiana General Assembly website, at http://iga.in.gov/legislative/2022/publications/agency_report/.

21. A list of Indiana state agencies and links to their websites can be found on the "Indiana Government and State Documents" research guide from the Jerome Hall Law Library, https://law.indiana.libguides.com/INDocs.

IV. Federal Administrative Research

You fill find that Indiana's administrative process closely follows the federal model. This section will briefly highlight the quasi-legislative and quasi-judicial functions of federal agencies, and the available resources for researching their documents.

A. Federal Regulations

Similar to Indiana's process, the general rulemaking process at the federal level requires an agency to publish a proposed rule, referred to as a notice of proposed rulemaking (NPRM); allow for a notice-and-comment period of typically 30–60 days; and consider and respond to the public comments before publishing a final draft of the regulation. The federal Administrative Procedure Act is found at 5 U.S.C. § 551 et seq. Section 553 provides the rulemaking process; section 554 provides the adjudicative process.

Federal regulations are published in two publications. Proposed rules, final rules, other agency notices, and select presidential documents are published in the *Federal Register*, a daily publication organized alphabetically by agency. Once finalized, final rules are codified and published in a second publication, the *Code of Federal Regulations* (CFR). The *Code of Federal Regulations* is published annually, in quarterly installments.[22] If you are citing to the current version of a final regulation, when possible, cite to the *Code of Federal Regulations*.

The *Federal Register* serves as a better research tool for understanding the history and context for a particular federal regulation. In addition to the regulatory text, proposed and final rules in the *Federal Register* include a preamble that provides a wealth of additional information related to the regulation, such as background information on the purpose behind a new regulation, the history of a particular regulatory scheme, and details on the regulation's fiscal and environmental impact. The *Code of Federal Regulations*, on the other hand, contains just the text of the final, codified regulations. However, the advantage of a codified set of regulations is that they are arranged topically, whereas regulations in the *Federal Register* are only published chronologically.

---

22. Titles 1–16 are updated as of January 1; titles 17–27 are updated as of April 1; titles 28–41 are updated as of July 1; and titles 42–50 are updated as of October 1.

Both the *Federal Register* and the *Code of Federal Regulations* are published and available in print, but you can also find them online, in both free and commercial services. Table 8-3 shows the availability of these publications on govinfo.gov, Lexis, and Westlaw.

Table 8-3. Federal Regulations on Govinfo, Lexis and Westlaw

	Govinfo.gov	Lexis	Westlaw
Federal Register	Current and archive back to 1936 (inception)	Current and archive back to 1936 (inception)	Current and archive back to 1936 (inception)
Code of Federal Regulations	Current and archive back to 1996	Current and archive back to 1981	Current and archive back to 1984

B. Researching Federal Regulations on Govinfo.gov and Related Government Websites

There are several excellent government websites that provide access to federal regulations. Govinfo.gov is a central clearinghouse of federal government documents. As Table 8-3 shows, govinfo.gov includes both the *Federal Register* and the *Code of Federal Regulations*. You can browse or search either publication, and while the site lacks any editorial enhancements, there are a couple of noteworthy features: First and foremost, the digitized versions of the *Federal Register* and the *Code of Federal Regulations* available here are official, authenticated government documents. Second, govinfo.gov provides access to several finding aids that can assist your regulatory research, including the "CFR Parts Affected," which shows where new regulations will fit in the codified collection; and a "Parallel Table of Authorities and Rules for the CFR and the US Code," which is helpful if you are trying to track down the statutory authority for a particular regulation.

For researching in the *Federal Register* specifically, another superb site is federalregister.gov. This site is a website version of the *Federal Register*. It provides quick access to each daily issue, as well as the ability to search past issues by keyword, date, citation, agency, and more. When you pull up a regulation on federalregister.gov, it is in an unofficial format, but offers links to the authenticated version from govinfo.gov. If you are conducting a regulatory history and want to see what types of comments the agency received for a particular regulation, federalregister.gov also links to the regulatory docket, available from regulations.gov.[23] Finally, federalregister.gov contains a feature called "Public Inspection," which provides a preview of the next day's issue; for those who closely monitor regulatory activity, this can be a very helpful feature. If you are doing significant regulatory research, another advantage of federalregister.gov is the ability to create a free My FR account, where you can save and annotate your research.[24]

Finally, because the *Code of Federal Regulations* is updated annually in quarterly installments, it takes some time for newly finalized regulations to be published in their codified form; thus the official current version of the *Code of Federal Regulations* rarely contains all finalized rules. Another resource that has been created to assist with this issue is the Electronic Code of Federal Regulations, or e-CFR.[25] This version of the CFR adds final rules from the *Federal Register* to the e-CFR database on a daily basis, to create a continually updated, but unofficial, version of the CFR.

C. Researching Federal Regulations on Westlaw

From the Westlaw home page, access federal regulations by clicking on "Regulations," then under Federal, "Code of Federal Regulations." Here you can search or browse by title. Under "Tools & Resources" on the right, Westlaw also provides the "Code of Federal Regulations Index," helpful if you are struggling to find the right keyword for the search you are trying to perform. An added advantage to regulatory research on Westlaw is access to the citator, for case annotations (Notes of Decisions), citing references, and history documents. To access the *Federal Register* on Westlaw, from the "Federal materials" tab, click on "Federal Register." From there you can search all *Federal Register* issues back to its inception. Unlike the CFR, no citator information is available for the *Federal Register.*

---

23. This site is also where you can go to submit a comment on a proposed regulation.

24. This is similar to the foldering option on Lexis or Westlaw.

25. The website is https://ecfr.gov.

D. Researching Federal Regulations on Lexis

From the Lexis home page, click on "Administrative Codes," then "Federal." From here, you can search both the *Code of Federal Regulations* and the *Federal Register* simultaneously or click on a particular publication to search individually. You can search or browse the *Code of Federal Regulations* by title. You have access to citator information on regulations in the *Code of Federal Regulations*, through the tabs at the top of the document or by clicking the "Shepardize document" link on the right. You can also compare regulatory text by clicking the "Compare Versions" button to compare one year's CFR to another. You can search the *Federal Register* or browse it by year. There is no citator information available for regulations in the *Federal Register*.

E. Researching Federal Regulations on Bloomberg Law

From the Bloomberg Law home page, click on the Browse menu, select "Laws & Regulations," then "Code of Federal Regulations." From here you can search or browse the CFR. Alternatively, from "Laws & Regulations," select "Regulatory Resources" to search regulations more broadly. This page will allow you to search both the CFR and the *Federal Register*, and is another avenue for accessing an individual state's regulations or all state regulations, helpful if you are conducting comparative regulatory research. Bloomberg Law's Smart Code® feature is available for regulatory research in the CFR but not the *Federal Register*.

V. Federal Agency Materials

A. Administrative Decisions

Federal agencies with quasi-judicial powers will issue written opinions at the conclusion of formal adjudicative proceedings. These opinions are often non-precedential, but binding on the immediate parties involved, and can be highly persuasive in later administrative disputes. There are several places you might look to locate federal administrative opinions. Some agencies, like some courts, publish their own official reporter of administrative decisions. There are also commercial publishers who specialize in publishing administrative decisions, chiefly, the Commerce Clearinghouse (CCH), and the Bureau of National Affairs (BNA). In print, these reporters often closely resemble case reporters, in hardbound volumes; some are published in what is known as a looseleaf format, where each volume is in a binder, and new pages (leaves) can be added or removed as needed. This is a much faster method of updating print resources.

Electronically, there are several subscription-based services that provide access to administrative decisions. CCH, through Wolters Kluwer, has a platform called VitalLaw that provides access to its administrative publications. BNA, recently acquired by Bloomberg Law, provides access to its administrative reporters through the Bloomberg Law platform. Westlaw and Lexis also provide access to administrative decisions from over fifty agencies. HeinOnline additionally provides access to digitized versions of the official reports of federal agencies.

Today many agencies post their most recent administrative decisions on their own websites. The National Labor Relations Board, as a shining example, provides access to not only recent Board and Administrative Law Judge decisions, but even the full docket for recent and ongoing cases.[26]

B. Judicial Opinions

The judiciary can play a crucial role in understanding administrative law as well, so it is important to note that, as you conduct administrative law research, you may come across judicial decisions that bear on your research. If you are researching a regulation, regulatory disputes arise commonly in litigation, so you may find that citing references to a regulation in Lexis, Westlaw, or Bloomberg Law lead you to relevant judicial opinions. Likewise, administrative adjudications at the agency level can be appealed up into the court system, once all administrative remedies have been exhausted. At the federal level, agency administrative appeals go to the relevant geographic Court of Appeals for the parties involved or to the Court of Appeals for the Federal Circuit.

---

26. NLRB Board decisions go back to volume 1 of their official reporter, which began in 1935, available at https://www.nlrb.gov/cases-decisions/decisions/board-decisions. Administrative Law Judge decisions go back to 1992, available at https://www.nlrb.gov/cases-decisions/decisions/administrative-law-judge-decisions.

C. Agency Guidance Documents

Federal agencies publish a host of advisory, interpretive, and explanatory documents, intended to provide guidance to the public in understanding their regulatory schemes. These guidance documents can range from annual reports to newsletters to circulars and bulletins, which are often technical in nature, providing specifics on new or amended programs within the agency. Finally, agency manuals and handbooks, drafted for employees of the agency, can be helpful to the public as well in better understanding how the agency operates.

Commercial services like Lexis and Westlaw provide access to some of these materials, particularly manuals, but one of the best resources for locating an agency's own publications is the agency's website. If you are having difficulty locating the website of a federal agency, USA.gov has an agency index that will help you find the correct website.[27]

VI. Attorney General Opinions

The attorney general at the state or federal level offers legal advice and interpretation to inquiring governmental bodies. The opinions they author are non-precedential, but highly persuasive. Indiana's attorney general opinions are available for free from the state website, back to 2001.[28] Lexis and Westlaw each have longer collections of Indiana attorney general opinions, back to 1953 and 1977, respectively. At the federal level, United States Attorney General opinions were originally published in a collection titled *Official Opinions of the Attorneys General of the United States*, which began publication in 1791. Authority was later delegated to the Office of Legal Counsel, which began publishing its attorney general opinions in *Opinions of the Office of Legal Counsel* in 1977. The full range of U.S. Attorney General opinions are available on Lexis, Westlaw, and HeinOnline. All published opinions of the Office of Legal Counsel are available from the Office's website, as well as select opinions back to 1934. Table 8-4 provides a description of the holdings for

---

27. A-Z Index of U.S. Government Departments and Agencies, https://www.usa. gov/federal-agencies.

28. Available at https://www.in.gov/attorneygeneral/about-the-office/ advisory-and-opinions/.

Indiana Attorney General opinions and U.S. Attorney General Opinions on government websites, Lexis, Westlaw, and HeinOnline.

Table 8-4. Attorney General Opinions Online

	.gov	Lexis	Westlaw	HeinOnline
Indiana AGO	IN.gov, back to 2001	Current and archive back to 1953	Current and archive back to 1977	Current and archive back to 1873
U.S. DOJ AGO	justice.gov/olc, all published decisions back to 1977, select back to 1934	Current and archive back to 1791	Current and archive back to 1791	Current and archive back to 1791

VII. Executive Orders & Proclamations

Before concluding this chapter, it is worth noting two other administrative documents that have the force of law: executive orders and proclamations, issued by the president at the federal level and the governor at the state level. Executive orders are typically directed at the executive branch of the government, often one or more agencies, and may even be used to create a new agency. Proclamations today are more commemorative, providing details on things such as holidays and federal observances. A third category here, administrative orders, which can come in the form of memos, notices, letters, and messages, focus on the administrative functioning of the government.

At the federal level, each of these documents is published in the *Federal Register*; because they have the force of law, executive orders and proclamations are also published in Title 3 of the *Code of Federal Regulations*. You can therefore also find these orders and proclamations on federalregister.gov and govinfo.gov. In addition, you can find the executive orders of the latest administration on the White House website.[29] Commercial services such as

---

29. Available at https://www.whitehouse.gov/briefing-room/presidential-actions/.

Lexis and Westlaw have large collections of presidential documents as well, typically categorized under the Executive Office of the President.

Indiana executive orders for the current governor can be found on the governor's website.[30] Archived pages of two previous gubernatorial administrations provide access to an archive of Indiana executive orders back to 2005.[31]

---

30. Available at https://www.in.gov/gov/newsroom/executive-orders/.

31. For Governor Mitch Daniels, EO's from 2005 to 2012, available at https://www.in.gov/governorhistory/mitchdaniels/2400.htm. For Governor Mike Pence, EO's from 2013 to 2016, available at https://www.in.gov/governorhistory/mikepence/2384.htm.

Chapter 9

Bill Tracking and Legislative History Research

I. The Legislative Process & Legislative Publications

Lawyers, federal and state agencies, and courts frequently use legislative history to divine the intention behind ambiguous statutes and to support their preferred interpretation of the statutory text. Legislative history documents are secondary sources and do not have the force of law. Whether they should be relied upon to determine congressional intent remains a topic of considerable debate. In order to find legislative history materials, you must have a basic understanding of the legislative process. Almost every stage of the legislative process produces legislative history materials. Compiling a legislative history involves collecting the documents produced throughout the different stages of the legislative process. Typical documents included in legislative history research are committee reports, draft and final bills and resolutions, legislative journals, and hearing and debate transcripts. When looking for evidence of legislative intent, the document usually accorded the most weight is the committee report.[1] After the committee report, in descending order of influence, are congressional floor debates and remarks, followed by the various bill versions, then congressional hearings and statements of witnesses, committee prints, and finally the markup amendments and other documents produced in committee. This chapter describes how laws are made by the Indiana General Assembly and the U.S. Congress with details about the types of documents produced at each stage of the law-making

---

1. Or the bill's conference report, if it ended up being referred to a conference committee.

process. It also covers how to monitor proposed legislation at the state and federal levels.

A. Indiana's Legislative Process

The legislative process in Indiana is similar to that of the federal system; see Table 9-1 for details. Indiana has a bicameral legislature consisting of the Indiana House of Representatives and the Indiana Senate. Collectively, they are referred to as the General Assembly. The Indiana House of Representatives has 100 members, each of whom is elected to a two-year term. The Indiana Senate has 50 members who serve four-year terms. The Indiana General Assembly is a part-time legislature. It meets for sixty-one days in odd-numbered years and thirty days during even-numbered years. Standard General Assembly sessions occur over two consecutive years, but special sessions may be convened at the discretion of the Governor. If a bill fails to pass by the end of the legislative session in which it was introduced, it is defunct and must be re-introduced in a subsequent session and go through the full legislative process again before it can become a law.

Table 9-1. Indiana Legislative Process

Steps of the Indiana Legislative Process
1. The language of a proposed bill is drafted by a legislator's office, usually with assistance from the Legislative Services Agency.
2. The bill is introduced by a legislator in his or her chamber and assigned to a standing committee. Once introduced, a bill is labeled. The first two letters designate the chamber in which the bill originated and the numbers are chronologically assigned.[2]
3. The assigned standing committee(s) hold hearings where they approve, amend, or reject the bill. The Indiana General Assembly's website has a list of all standing committees. For each committee you can view the bills they have been assigned for the current legislative session.[3]
4. At the conclusion of the hearings, a report containing the Committee's recommendation is returned to the chamber in which the bill originated.

---

2. *E.g.*, SB 209 indicates that this bill was the 209th bill introduced in the Senate during that session.

3. To access, from the Indiana General Assembly's website, go to the Committees tab > Standing.

5. The originating chamber then considers the bill and it is eligible for a second reading and, if passed, a third reading. During this time the bill can be amended in accordance with the Committee's recommendations or as legislators deem appropriate. Once a bill has passed the second reading it becomes an engrossed bill. During the third reading legislative debates may occur over the bill's merits and a roll call vote is taken. Within the originating chamber, passage requires approval by a simple majority.

6. If passed, the approved version of the bill is sent over to the other legislative chamber for consideration. The non-originating chamber follows the same process of referral to committee and first, second, and third readings.

7. If the non-originating chamber amends the bill it is then referred to a joint conference committee composed of House and Senate members. The conference committee works to amend the language to the satisfaction of both the House and Senate. The bill is then returned to each chamber for another vote.

8. Once a version of the bill has passed both chambers it is called an enrolled act.

9. The enrolled act is then sent to the Office of the Attorney General which reviews it for constitutionality before it's presented to the Governor. The governor has the option of signing the act into law or, absent his or her signature, it becomes law after seven days of gubernatorial inaction. If the governor vetoes the measure, the legislature can override the veto by a majority vote in each chamber.

10. Each enrolled act is printed and bound in the *Indiana Acts*, the state's session law publication.

B. Indiana's Statutory Publication Process

Both federal and state jurisdictions share the same publication path for statutes: from slip law to session law to the codified version, and, ultimately, to inclusion in an annotated code. Slip laws are paper prints of the public and private laws enacted by the legislature. The General Assembly, Indiana's state legislature, meets every year. Standard General Assembly sessions occur over two consecutive years, but special sessions may be convened at the discretion of the Governor. At the conclusion of each biennial or special session, all of the laws passed during the session are organized chronologically and published in the *Laws of the state of Indiana: passed and published, at the ... session of the General Assembly*, commonly referred to as the *Indiana Acts*. Each session law is assigned a number based on the order it passed the General Assembly, which combined with the year, provides its citation (e.g., the first enacted public law in 2019 was designated as P.L. 1-2019.). The effective date of all new laws is July 1 during the year it passed, unless the enrolled act contains a provision to the contrary.

Starting with the 2nd Regular Session of the 111th Indiana General Assembly in 2000, *Indiana Acts* are available online at the legislature's website.[4] Click on the "Laws" tab and select "Acts" from the dropdown list. On the left is a menu where you can select the year you wish to view. Finding aids to help researchers are included at the end of each volume: a "Table of Citations Affected" indicates each section of the Code impacted by legislation enacted during the session; the "Bill Numbers to Public Law Numbers" table cross-references House and Senate bill numbers to their respective public law numbers for the session; and the "Public Law Numbers to Bill Numbers" table does the reverse—matching House and Senate public law numbers to bill numbers. For each set of session laws, a subject index is also included.

II. Indiana Bill Tracking

Bill tracking is the method of monitoring the status of the current bill as it makes its way through the legislative process. You may be interested in a bill for a couple of reasons—perhaps you need information about pending legislation to properly advise a client or you may represent someone interested in influencing the outcome of a proposed bill. Pending legislation may also be helpful to determine the legislative intent of a previously enacted statute.

Tracing current Indiana bills can be accomplished using the General Assembly's website. Find the specific legislation you are seeking and the site provides details about actions taken on the bill, the current and prior versions, any amendments, information about who introduced the measure, and results of any votes that have taken place. There are also commercial services that track state-level legislation. For example, Indiana Bill Tracking in Lexis contains a summary and legislative chronology of all pending Indiana legislation in the current legislative session and prior sessions back to 1989.

---

4. Available at http://iga.in.gov/.

III. Sources of Indiana Legislative History

In Indiana, the state's legislative history materials are limited to: (1) House and Senate bills and resolutions; (2) House and Senate Journals; (3) statutory publications (i.e., state session laws and *Indiana Code*); and (4) selected reports. Indiana General Assembly floor debates are not recorded in print.[5] The *Brevier Legislative Reports* are a historical exception. Between 1858 and 1887, transcripts were made of the speeches and debates that occurred on the floor of the House and Senate. These volumes were digitized by the Jerome Hall Law Library at Indiana University's Maurer School of Law with the help of a grant from the Institute of Museum and Library Sciences.[6]

A. Bills and Resolutions—Indiana

Bills tend to be the easiest legislative document to find. For current bills and resolutions in Indiana's General Assembly, go to the legislature's website and click on the "Legislation" tab. Select "Bills" or "Resolutions" depending upon the content you're seeking. If you don't know the number of the bill but want to find a bill on a particular topic, select "By Subject" to access the "Legislative Subject Index" for the current session.[7] For each bill you can see current and prior versions, any amendments made by either chamber, a description of the bill, outcomes of roll call votes, and fiscal notes. The General Assembly's site has an archive which contains bills from prior sessions dating back to 2000. As an alternative, Lexis also has the full text of all bills introduced in the General Assembly (with mark ups showing amendments made) from 1991 to present in its "Indiana Full Text Bills" collection.

B. House and Senate Journals—Indiana

Each chamber of Indiana's General Assembly produces a daily publication of the activities in their respective chamber. These journals include the text of

---

5. While not available in print, records of both committee and floor consideration of bills from 2000 to present may be available via video, http://iga.in.gov/information/archives/. Painstaking though it can be to watch hours of legislative debate, if such video coverage is available for the bill you are researching, this can be a way of discerning legislative intent in Indiana.

6. Available online at: https://law.indiana.edu/lawlibrary/collections/other-digital-collections.html.

7. For example, if you were researching a topic related to art therapy, you might look for pending legislation under the topic "Artists and Art."

bills and resolutions that have been introduced, voting outcomes, legislators' statements, committee recommendations on pending bills, and much more. Recent General Assembly House and Senate Journals can be accessed on the legislature's website[8] by clicking on the "Session" tab and selecting "Daily Journals" under either the Senate or House. The Journals are fully searchable and can be downloaded or printed. For Journals prior to 2014, click the "Session" link under "Archives 2000–2013." Select the "Additional Documents" link for the legislative session you are interested in and there will be a link to a PDF version of the Journals in the list. Historical Indiana House and Senate Journals can also be found online or in print at several law libraries throughout Indiana, including the Indiana State Library. The legislative journals have indexes which can be searched by subject. This feature is particularly helpful if you don't know the bill number of the legislation you are researching. Table 9-2 provides a list of locations for accessing Indiana House and Senate Journals online.

Table 9-2. Sources for Indiana House and Senate Journals

Location	Coverage	URL
Indiana General Assembly	House (2004–current)	iga.in.gov
	Senate (2005–current)	
Internet Archive	(1816–1879)	archive.org
Indiana State Library's Digital Collections	House (1817–1879)	digitalcollections.library.in.gov
	Senate (1818–1875)	
HathiTrust	sporadic	hathitrust.org

C. Legislative Reports—Indiana

The Indiana Legislative Services Agency (ILSA) is an agency of the General Assembly which provides fiscal analysis and legislative research services to the Indiana legislature. Select reports from the mid-1990s to present produced by ILSA and other agencies in connection with proposed legislation are available under the "Publications" tab on the General Assembly's website.

---

8. The website is http://iga.in.gov/.

D. Session Laws—Indiana

The easiest way to begin researching state legislative history is to start with a session law.[9] Session laws are a chronological arrangement of all laws passed in a particular legislative session, including acts which have not been codified. Each session law contains references to the bill number assigned to the legislation, which can then be used to find related legislative documents. Refer to Chapter 4 on "Constitutions, Statutes, and Court Rules" in this book for resources and strategies for finding session laws.

IV. Researching Other States' Legislative History

Availability of state legislative history documents varies greatly between jurisdictions.[10] Online access is typically quite limited and printed records are not widely held. When they exist, government libraries, public law libraries, and state archives are the most likely repositories for these materials. The Jerome Hall Law Library at Indiana University's Maurer School of Law has created an excellent research guide on "State Legislative History Research."[11] There is a related guide "Compiling State Legislative Histories (with information on Indiana Legislative documents)" which is also helpful.[12] In addition AALL's Government Documents—Special Interest Section produces "State Bibliographies" which consist of bibliographic lists of each state's law-related documents and publications.[13]

---

9. Tip: Consult Bluebook table T1.3 to find the official title of each state's session laws.

10. To find a listing of legislative history guides that can assist you in researching other states' legislation, check out the "Inventory of State Legislative History Research Guides" at https://law.indiana.libguides.com/state-legislative-history-guides.

11. *Id.*

12. Available at https://law.indiana.libguides.com/compiling-state-legislative-histories.

13. Available in Spinelli's Law Librarian's Reference Shelf on HeinOnline.

V. Federal Legislative Research Process

The United States legislature meets in two-year cycles. That time period is referred to as a "Congress." Each year of the cycle is a separate congressional session. During the congressional session, members of the House and Senate introduce proposed legislation (i.e., a bill or joint resolution). When a bill is introduced, a brief summary, text of the bill, and commentary connected with the introduction of the bill are published in the *Congressional Record*.[14] It is also assigned a bill number.[15] A bill's text can be helpful in determining congressional intent, particularly when comparing original and subsequent versions of the legislation. You can examine the edits made to the bill's provisions to determine possible goals and rationale. Keep in mind, however, that the bill text shouldn't be viewed in isolation when determining legislative intent. The savvy researcher will evaluate it in light of the other legislative history documents they've found.

The bill is then referred to a committee (sometimes more than one). Committees are tasked with gathering information about the proposed legislation, including any positive or negative outcomes if the legislation is passed. To facilitate this process, the assigned committee may hold hearings on the merits of approving, amending, or rejecting the bill.[16] These hearings include testimony from experts, interested parties, and others who may be impacted by the legislation. Hearing documents include transcripts of such testimony, as well as any underlying documents (reports, studies, etc.) that have been submitted to the committee. Hearing information contains valuable insights into the different arguments for and against the bill. Hearings also impact the ultimate conclusion of the committee and its report. There is a months-long publication lag for hearing materials, but archived videos of the hearing and statements prepared in advance and submitted to the committee are often available much sooner. Hearing transcripts are not included in the *Congressional Record*; however, commercial services, such as *CQ Transcripts*, do

---

14. Content published when a bill is introduced varies by chamber. Regardless, at a minimum, the bill's number and title, its sponsors, and the committee(s) it was referred to will be included in the *Congressional Record*.

15. Bill numbers are assigned based upon the chamber they originated in and the order in which they were proposed during the session. For example, the first bill introduced in the Senate during a session would be S. 1, the next S. 2, and so forth.

16. Whether to hold hearings is within the discretion of the committee. As a result, many bills "die in committee" due to inaction.

provide transcripts of testimony from congressional hearings. In addition to hearings, committees sometimes obtain special studies called "committee prints" about subjects related to the bill. These can provide useful insights into the policies and issues related to the committee's evaluation of the proposed legislation.

Sometimes committees will schedule a "markup" meeting to amend the bill by committee vote before referring it to the full chamber. These amended bills aren't officially published but are sometimes accessible on the committee's website. If a majority of the committee votes in favor of a bill, it is sent to the full House or Senate along with its committee report. Committee reports are considered one of the most valuable types of legislative history documents. These reports contain background and other information about the proposed legislation.[17] The *Congressional Record* does not publish committee reports, but logs when the bill comes out of committee and provides a citation to the report.[18]

Once a bill has met with committee approval, it is brought before the entire chamber for debate and consideration. Transcripts of floor debates are published verbatim in the *Congressional Record*. These statements provide good insight into congressional intent in passing a particular bill. If a bill passes in the chamber in which it was introduced, it then goes over to the other chamber for consideration, voting, and possible passage. If the Senate and House pass versions of the bill that are different, it is referred to a conference committee that works to blend them into a single bill that can be approved by both chambers. The bill is then sent back to the House and Senate to be voted on by each. Bills that aren't passed by both chambers before the two-year Congress ends "die" and do not roll over to the next session.[19] If a bill passes both the House and the Senate, it is considered an enrolled bill, and presented to the President for signing. The President must sign or veto the bill within ten days. A vetoed bill may be overridden by a two-thirds vote of both the House and Senate. If the President fails to take any action within that ten-day period, the bill becomes law without signature. If the

---

17. Types of information that may be included: fiscal impact, record of committee votes, analysis of effects on existing laws, and summaries of positive and dissenting viewpoints.

18. Committee reports are designated by H. Rept. (or S. Rept.) followed by <congressional session> - <sequentially assigned #> (e.g., H. Rept. 115-1129).

19. These bills must be reintroduced and go through the entire process again to have the chance of becoming law.

congressional session adjourns before the ten-day period expires and the President takes no action on the bill prior to adjournment, the bill dies and Congress cannot override it. This is known as a *pocket veto*.

Passed bills are assigned a public or private law number depending upon whether they apply to the general public or are specific to an individual or small group. Public and private law numbers are assigned in the order in which the bill was passed. For example, the first public law of the 116th Congress would be Pub. L. No. 116-1.

A. Compiled Federal Legislative Histories

Before digging into legislative history research and starting from scratch, find out if there is an existing compiled legislative history for that particular law. Federal legislative history compilations are available in a variety of commercial and free resources. Of these, the most robust is ProQuest's Legislative Insight database. It contains over 18,000 federal legislative histories with coverage back to 1929. Law Librarians' Society of Washington, D.C. has pulled together lists of free and commercially available legislative histories: "Legislative Histories of Selected U.S. Laws on the Internet: Free Sources"[20] and "Legislative Histories of Selected U.S. Laws on the Internet: Commercial Sources."[21] Researchers can also use Nancy Johnson's *Sources of Compiled Legislative Histories: A Bibliography of Government Documents, Periodical Articles, and Books* to find additional sources for legislative history. *Sources of Compiled Legislative Histories* is available in print and in the "U.S. Federal Legislative History Library" in HeinOnline.[22] Another solid resource for collections of legislative history is the *United States Code Congressional and Administrative News* (USCCAN), which is available on Westlaw.[23] USCCAN doesn't provide comprehensive or complete legislative histories, but it provides a researcher a good foundation to build upon.

---

20. The website is https://www.llsdc.org/legislative-histories-laws-on-the-internet -free-sources.

21. The website is https://www.llsdc.org/lh-of-us-laws-on-the-internet-commer-cial-sources.

22. Resource also includes federal legislative histories published by the U.S. Government Printing Office and others.

23. Proposed & Enacted Legislation > under Tools & Resources: Legislative History > under Federal: U.S. Code Congressional & Administrative News

B. Federal Bill Tracking

You can track federal legislation for free using Congress.gov.[24] Select the bill you want to track and click the "get alerts" link next to the congressional session (note that it requires creation of a free account on the site). GovTrack.us also has free tracking features.[25] Note that it's run by a non-profit and is not an official government site.

C. Federal Statutory Publication

At the conclusion of each Congressional session, that session's slip laws are organized chronologically by date of passage and bound into volumes called the *United States Statutes at Large*. These are referred to as "session laws" because they are published at the end of the legislative session. In addition to all public and private laws enacted during the session, the *Statutes at Large* includes concurrent resolutions, any proposed and ratified constitutional amendments, and presidential proclamations. A statute can be referred to by its *Statutes at Large* citation or by its public law number (e.g., Pub. L. No. 94-553 or 90 Stat. 2541).

For public laws, the volume and page where the law will eventually appear in the *Statutes at Large* is included at the top of the Act.[26] Private laws only receive their statutory citations at the time they are added to the *Statutes at Large* because of their limited applicability. The header and side notes of each slip law contain its public (or private) law number, the date of enactment, bill number, popular name of the law (if any), and—*for public laws only*—its U.S. Code citations and legislative history. In addition to the print publication, complete runs of the *U.S. Statutes at Large* are available in a number of commercial databases, including Westlaw, Lexis, HeinOnline, and LLMC Digital. Free and open access is also available through the Library of Congress[27] and the Government Publishing Office (GPO),[28] with coverage from 1789 through 2016. Conducting legal research in the *Statutes at Large* is challenging due to its chronological arrangement. Related topics are not collocated, which necessitates extensive cross-referencing, and there is no purging of laws that are no

---

24. The website is https://www.congress.gov/.
25. The website is https://www.govtrack.us/.
26. Public law means the act affects the whole of society, as distinguished from private laws which impact only an individual or small group.
27. Available at https://www.loc.gov/collections/united-states-statutes-at-large/about-this-collection/.
28. Available at https://www.govinfo.gov/.

longer in effect. Federal and state codes were developed to combat this problem. Grouping topically-related laws together makes finding all applicable statutes a much simpler endeavor. Codes are subject arrangements of the laws in effect within a jurisdiction. To achieve this reorganization, session laws undergo a process known as codification. Codification helps keep the law current by eliminating repealed or expired statutes and incorporating amendments to the original statute within the same code section. Codification of federal statutes is done by the Office of Law Revision Counsel.[29]

---

29. Available at https://uscode.house.gov/.

Chapter 10

Research Strategies

Law has a wealth of primary and secondary sources, which can be simultaneously helpful and overwhelming. When preparing to conduct legal research, therefore, it is beneficial to approach it with a plan. Whether you are researching for an article or for a case you are working on, think first, research later. Dissect your research scenario and figure out what legal issues you are going to be researching, and whether there may be legally significant facts as well. Distinguishing between issues of fact and issues of law can be challenging, but ultimately beneficial. An issue of law is law itself (e.g., negligence, battery, products liability, etc.), while an issue of fact is another factor in the legal scenario that could affect how the law is assessed (e.g., age of the parties, date of the incident, extent of damage, etc.). Brainstorming all of the potential legal and factual issues can help you create a research plan. Having a plan, knowing what specifically you want to research, will make your research much more efficient.

I. Consider Starting with a Secondary Source

It is also a good idea to think about where you want to start. Finding the law itself is your number one goal, but law librarians often recommend starting with a secondary source rather than a primary source. As discussed in Chapter 3, secondary sources provide background and context, and will point you toward key primary sources, such as cases and statutes, to expand your research. If you are unsure what keywords to use in your searches, what facts might be legally significant in your research, or what other legal issues you should be researching, secondary sources will often lead you in the right direction.

Deciding what secondary source to start with will depend on a number of factors. If the area of law you are researching is entirely new to you, you might want to start with a legal encyclopedia. As you will recall from Chapter 3, legal encyclopedias offer quick, general backgrounds on a variety of legal topics, and are written for a broad audience, so they are easy to understand. If you need more detail on the subtle complexities of a niche legal issue within a broader area of law, you might instead turn to a legal treatise, which goes into greater description and analysis than a legal encyclopedia. Regardless of where you start, once you find relevant articles in one secondary source, you can easily transition to another. If you have accessed your secondary source on a research database like Lexis or Westlaw, their editorial features will recommend additional secondary sources, topically linked, to expand your research.

Even if you are researching in print, once you find a relevant article in one secondary source, you can more easily transition to the same topic in another secondary source, using a couple of simple strategies. First, identify where your article of interest appears in that secondary source, then look to the source's table of contents to see, more broadly, how the content is organized, and where your article fits in that organizational scheme. Chances are good that other secondary sources in law will follow similar organization patterns, so you should be able to identify where, in the next source, you should look to find articles on your topic of interest by comparing the sources' tables of contents.

Second, once you find an article on the topic you are researching, take note of the terms that article uses to describe and discuss your topic. When you move to another secondary source to expand your research, you can seek out those terms in the index to that new secondary source, to look for further articles on your topic. Indexes use a controlled vocabulary to note where specific terms appear in their resource, so it is critical, when using such a tool, to think broadly of the different, related terms you might look for in the index, if your first term does not appear. If you are looking for laws related to dog owners, for example, you might first look for the term "dog," and if it is not listed in the index, instead try the synonym "canine" or the broader term "domesticated animal." The law tends to use particular terms to discuss and catalog specific legal issues or facts; once you start to recognize those terms, by reading them in various secondary sources, they become easier to identify as your research expands into additional sources.

II. Expanding Your Research into Primary Sources

When you get ready to conduct primary source research and track down the law itself, always make sure to see whether a statute applies to your legal scenario. It may not answer your question entirely, but if a statute governs your scenario, you must find it. You will then want to see how the courts have interpreted the statute. This is where an annotated code or the citator in Lexis or Westlaw will come in handy, as both will lead you to cases that have cited the statute. Recall from Chapter 6 that case annotations are editorially selected cases that have significantly interpreted a statute, whereas the citator will list all cases that have cited the statute.

As you dive into case law research, the factual issues you identified when you were planning your research can be a powerful tool, because you can look for cases that are similar to the facts of your research scenario. Legal research is rarely a one-case-fits-all journey; rather, it is more like a puzzle, where you pull from different pieces of law to assemble your complete picture. It is an iterative process that takes patience and organization.

III. Organizing Your Research

Speaking of organization, as you conduct your research, it is prudent to keep records of your research as you go along. There is no one right way to do this—whatever works best for you. Lexis and Westlaw, for instance, offer the ability to add documents to folders to save your research, but if you do not take notes on why you saved a particular case to a folder, you will find yourself having to re-read as your research continues. Make sure to annotate your saved resources to make the research process as efficient and smooth as possible.

The number one question when it comes to legal research is, "When do I stop?" It can be genuinely nerve-wracking wondering whether you have missed any cases in your research. Unfortunately, there is not a clear answer to that question. It gets easier with practice and experience, and there are some clues along the way. Make sure to cover your bases—do not just look at cases, but also look at statutes, and make sure there are no regulations or executive orders to deal with. Consult secondary sources to see if there are other perspectives on your legal issue that you need to explore. Case law research can often be the most stressful, but there are so many approaches to case law research that, if you employ multiple search techniques, you are likely to uncover any cases that did not pop up in your first search. If the same cases are coming up over and over in multiple searches, chances are that you have found the most important cases for your legal research question.

If you still have questions, all you have to do is ask! Law librarians are happy to help point you in the right direction. They cannot give legal advice (which includes finding "the best cases" for you), but they can recommend sources. In Indiana, we have three law school libraries, the Indiana Supreme Court Law Library, and the Vanderburgh County Law Library. Contact information is provided in Table 10-1.

Table 10-1. Law Libraries of Indiana

Name & Location	Contact Information
Indiana University Maurer School of Law Jerome Hall Law Library Bloomington, Indiana	Email: lawref@indiana.edu Chat: iub.libanswers.com/law Phone (812) 855-2938 Website: law.indiana.edu/lawlibrary
Indiana University McKinney School of Law Ruth Lilly Law Library Indianapolis, Indiana	Email: lawlref@iupui.edu Phone: (317) 274-4026 Website: mckinneylaw.iu.edu/library
Notre Dame Law School Kresge Law Library South Bend, Indiana	Email: askus@nd.edu Phone: (574) 631-7024 Website: law.nd.edu/library
Indiana Supreme Court Law Library Indianapolis, Indiana	Phone: (317) 232-2557 Website: in.gov/courts/supreme/law-library/
Vanderburgh County William H. Miller Law Library Evansville, Indiana	Email: kweston@vanderburghcounty.in.gov Phone: (812) 435-5175 Website: evansvillegov.org/county/topic/ index.php?topicid=249

Appendix A

Legal Citation

Authors include citations to materials they reference in their written works as a means of providing credit to the underlying source material. But citations are an important communication tool for the reader as well. A reader may look to cited material to expand their knowledge of a given topic, and a prudent researcher will look to cited material to verify the claims the citing author has made about the work before relying on those claims herself. Because citations serve such a powerful communicative role, it is important that the author provide sufficient information in the citation to enable a reader to easily track down the cited source. To address this, disciplines from the sciences to the humanities have developed citation systems to promote uniformity in the structure of citations, which not only aids the reader in interpreting the citation, but also the author in including all necessary components of the citation. Law is no exception. The most widely used legal citation system in the United States is *The Bluebook: A Uniform System of Citation* ["the *Bluebook*"]. Authors in law also often reference the *ALWD Guide to Legal Citation* ["the *ALWD Guide*"] for help formatting their citations; rather than a separate citation system, the principles of the *ALWD Guide* correspond to and reference the *Bluebook's* rules, while providing helpful explanation about some of the more confusing elements of legal citation.[1] It is worth noting here that some states have their own citation manuals as well, and still others may have citation guides written into their court rules. Indiana falls into the latter category; it does not have its own citation manual, but the *Indiana Rules of Appellate Procedure* provide a citation guide for certain types of legal documents, including cases, statutes, regulations, and court rules.[2] This

---

1. Ass'n of Legal Writing Dirs. & Carolyn V. Williams, *Preface*, in ALWD GUIDE TO LEGAL CITATION xxviii (7th ed. 2021).
2. IND. APP. RULE 22. The rule begins by saying that, "[u]nless otherwise provided, a current edition of a Uniform System of Citation (Bluebook) shall be followed."

appendix will highlight some of the most commonly cited legal materials, with references to the Indiana appellate rule on citation form, where appropriate, and will end with tips for efficient use of the *Bluebook* and the *ALWD Guide* for further citation assistance.

I. Understanding the Structure of the *Bluebook*

The *Bluebook* is written for different audiences of legal writers: The first section, the "Bluepages," offer the most basic rules of citation, and are designed for non-academic legal writing, such as briefs, memoranda, and other documents a legal practitioner might author. The second and largest section, the "Whitepages," dive deeper into legal citation, following the same basic structure of the citation rules provided in the Bluepages, but with some format variation, such as changes in typeface for certain elements in a legal citation. The Whitepages are designed for academic legal writing, such as books and law journal articles, and the rules outlined in the Whitepages offer more explanation and examples than those in the Bluepages; thus, the rules in the Bluepages often reference the rules in the Whitepages for further understanding of the citation format.[3] Another important difference, besides format, is location: in non-academic legal writing, citations typically appear in-text, while in academic legal writing, citations are typically provided as footnotes. Examples in this appendix will include both Bluepage and Whitepage formats for comparison.[4]

II. Citing Case Law

Bluebook rule B10 (Bluepages), *R10* (Whitepages); *ALWD rule 12.* Case citations are relatively formulaic and easy to understand, once you familiarize yourself with the basic components. A case citation includes the following elements: the case name, information about the reporter where the case was

---

3. The *ALWD Guide* likewise outlines citation variances between academic and non-academic legal writing, but does so within the same rule, rather than providing two separate sections of rules, as the *Bluebook* does. *ALWD Guide, supra* note 1, at xlvii.

4. Citations for any type of legal document can vary greatly in depth of complexity. This appendix will focus on the most basic formats for each type of featured legal document. For variances on this formula, refer to the referenced rules in the *Bluebook* or the *ALWD Guide*.

published, including the volume and page number, and the year of the decision.[5] In the case of *Hess v. Indiana*, for example, the full citation is: *Hess v. Indiana*, 414 U.S. 105 (1973). For an explanation of these elements and a comparison of the format variants, see Table A-1.

Table A-1. Case Citation

Citation Guide	Case Name	Volume Number	Reporter Abbreviation	Starting Page Number	Year of Decision
Bluebook Bluepages	Hess v. Indiana[6]	414	U.S.	105	(1973).
Bluebook Whitepages	Hess v. Indiana	414	U.S.	105	(1973).
Ind. App. Rule 22	*Hess v. Indiana*	414	U.S.	105	(1973).

III. Citing Statutes

Bluebook rule B12 (Bluepages); *R12* (Whitepages); *ALWD rule 14*. In most instances, when you cite a statute, you cite to its codified form. The format for a statutory citation varies by jurisdiction. In Indiana, you start with the name of the code, followed by four numbers: The title of the code, the article within that title, the chapter within that article, and finally the section within that chapter, representing the individual statute being cited; and ends with the year of the current print code.[7] For example, the Indiana law that sets the parameters allowing citizens to rescue animals from cars in limited dangerous circumstances (the so-called "Hot Dog" or "Good Samaritan" Law) is found at Indiana Code § 34-30-30-3 and would be cited using the formats outlined in Table A-2.

---

5. There can be variations from this format, for example, if a case opinion is only available online through a court's website. This is where reference to the rules in the *Bluebook* or the *ALWD Guide* can be of assistance. These rules will also go into great detail on the components of the citation, such as what to provide as the case name and how to deal with procedural phrases, such as "ex parte" and "ex rel."

6. May use italics rather than underline when following the Bluepages.

7. If citing an older version of the code, the date would come from that edition of the code or its pocket part or supplement, not the current edition.

Table A-2. Indiana Statute Citation

Citation Guide	Code Name	Section Symbol	Title	Article	Chapter	Section	Year
Bluebook Bluepages	Ind. Code	§	34-	30-	30-	3	(2020).
Bluebook Whitepages	IND. CODE	§	34-	30-	30-	3	(2020).
Ind. App. Rule 22	Ind. Code	§	34-	30-	30-	3	(2020).

IV. Citing Secondary Sources

Secondary sources can vary significantly in their citation formats, and while the *Bluebook* and *ALWD Guide* provide rules and examples for many common types of secondary sources, it would be impossible for them to cover every title or type of secondary source in their pages. Instead, authors must find the rule that most closely addresses the type of document they are trying to cite, and use that rule as a guide for creating their own citation.

A. Law Reviews & Journals

Bluebook rule B16 (Bluepages); *R16* (Whitepages); *ALWD rule 21*. Of the different types of secondary sources, law reviews are the most straightforward to cite. Similar to cases, law reviews follow a fairly steady formula for their citations. The biggest challenge can be determining how best to abbreviate the name of the journal. The *Bluebook* provides a number of tables following the Whitepages that can assist with this. Table T6, for example, lists "Common Words in Case Names, Institutional Author Names, and Periodical Titles." Correspondingly, the *ALWD Guide* offers similar abbreviations in Appendix 3(E), "Names of Cases, Institutional Authors, and Periodical Titles." Journal article citations include the following elements: author name, article title, journal name and information, including volume and starting page number, and year of publication. For an example of how a journal article citation would be structured, see Table A-3, showing the citation format for the *Indiana Law Journal* article, "First Amendment Investigations and the Inescapable Pragmatism of the Common Law of Free Speech."

Table A-3. Indiana Law Journal Citation

Citation Guide	Author	Article Title	Volume Number	Journal Title	Starting Page	Year of Publication
Bluebook Bluepages (followed by Ind. App. Rule 22)	Lawrence Rosenthal,	First Amendment Investigations and the Inescapable Pragmatism of the Common Law of Free Speech,[8]	86	Ind. L.J.	1	(2011).
Bluebook Whitepages	Lawrence Rosenthal,	*First Amendment Investigations and the Inescapable Pragmatism of the Common Law of Free Speech,*	86	IND. L.J.	1	(2011).

B. Encyclopedias

Bluebook rule B15 (Bluepages); *R15* (Whitepages); *ALWD rule 22.* The citation format for an encyclopedia depends on the publication format, for example, whether the encyclopedia entries are authored by the same person or multiple authors, and whether the encyclopedia comes in one vol-

---

8. Underlined or italicized.

ume or multiple volumes. To structure your encyclopedia citation using the *Bluebook*, follow the rule for books and other nonperiodic materials as a guide to creating your citation. If you have access to the *ALWD Guide*, it provides more examples specific to encyclopedias in its chapter on "Dictionaries, Encyclopedias, and *American Law Reports*." Depending on the format of the encyclopedia, your citation will contain at least some of the following elements: author or editor name, volume number, section number, and year. For an example, see Table A-4.

Table A-4. Encyclopedia Citation

Citation Guide	Author	Section Name	Volume Number	Encyclopedia Name	Section Number	Year
Bluebook Bluepages (followed by Ind. App. Rule 22)	Lonnie E. Griffith, Jr.,	*Immunity for Removing Domestic Animal from Locked Motor Vehicle, in*	1A	*Ind. Law Encyc.*	*Animals* § 5.50	(2021).
Bluebook Whitepages	Lonnie E. Griffith, Jr.,	*Immunity for Removing Domestic Animal from Locked Motor Vehicle, in*	1A	Ind. Law Encyc.	Animals § 5.50	(2021).

C. Treatises

Bluebook rule B15 (Bluepages); *R15* (Whitepages); *ALWD rule 20*. Both the *Bluebook* and the *ALWD Guide* place treatises within the basic rule for non-periodic materials. How you structure the citation depends entirely on how the treatise is published, for instance, whether the treatise is in one volume or spans multiple volumes. Because of the variety of formats, there is no one basic citation format for a treatise, though both the *Bluebook* and the *ALWD Guide* provide several illustrative examples you can follow in formatting your citation. At a minimum, you can expect to include an author or editor's name, the name of the chapter or section of your treatise, the title of the treatise, the volume (where appropriate), the edition (where appropriate), the starting page number, and the date of publication. For an example of how you would structure a citation to the *Indiana Practice Series*, see Table A-5.

Table A-5. Treatise Citation

Citation Guide	Volume Number	Author	Section Name	Treatise Title	Starting Page	Edition	Year
Bluebook Bluepages (followed by Ind. App. Rule 22)	3A	Stephen A. Arthur & William F. Harvey,	*Rules of Proc. Ann. R. 56, in*	Ind. Prac.,[9]	254	(3d ed.	2003).
Bluebook Whitepages	3A	STEPHEN A. ARTHUR & WILLIAM F. HARVEY,	*Rules of Proc. Ann. R. 56, in*	IND. PRAC.,	254	(3d ed.	2003).

_____

9. Underline or italics acceptable.

D. Other Secondary Sources

The sources highlighted above represent only a fraction of the secondary sources you might need to cite according to the rules of the *Bluebook* or *ALWD Guide*. And as noted in the section on treatises, there is no one reliable formula for structuring a citation to any secondary source. If you are struggling to format your citation, here are a couple of tips:

- **Check the index.** Both the *Bluebook* and the *ALWD Guide* have thorough indexes, so you might try flipping through the index pages to look for assistance. Depending on the source you are trying to cite, you might look for index entries based on the title of the publication or the type of publication. If you are citing a popular source with a national scope, there may be a specific citation rule just for that title. This is rare, but worth a look. For example, the *American Law Reports* has its own *Bluebook* rule, R16.7.7 (Whitepages) and *ALWD* rule, 22.5. If the title of your publication does not have its own index entry, however, you might look through the index for the type of publication instead, such as treatise, encyclopedia, dictionary, or restatement. This will help direct you to the proper rule, where you can use the examples and explanations provided to create your own citation.

- **Think about the features of your publication.** If you are still struggling to properly format your citation, remember the purpose of citation and think about the features of your publication as a means to identify what needs to be included. Is there an author and/or an editor? Is the publication one volume or several? Has the publication been published in more than one edition? What is the year of publication? Identifying the answers to all of these questions will help you pick the best examples to follow from the *Bluebook* or *ALWD* rule and compose your citation.

V. Helpful Features in the *Bluebook* and the *ALWD Guide*

Composing proper legal citations is not always easy. However, in addition to the rules themselves, the *Bluebook* and the *ALWD Guide* include several features to help make citation a less painful process.

A. The Best of the *Bluebook*

- Quick Reference Guides

Because the *Bluebook* includes different citation formats for academic and nonacademic writing, it provides separate quick reference guides for each style. These guides include examples of the most frequently cited legal materials (such as cases, statutes, and periodicals), without all the explanation found in the pages of the rules themselves, serving as a convenient tool for fast citation work. The "Quick Reference Guide for Law Review (Academic) Footnotes," corresponding to the Whitepages, is found in the inside front cover and first page of the *Bluebook,* and the "Quick Reference" guide for non-academic publications, corresponding to the Bluepages, can be found on the last page and inside back cover.

- Tables

Another prominent feature of the *Bluebook* is the array of tables found toward the back of the publication. These are helpful supplements to the *Bluebook* rules, assisting with such things as identifying the most authoritative source within a jurisdiction to cite to, as well as providing guides to commonly cited words and how best to abbreviate them. Particular tables of note include "T1: United States Jurisdictions," which starts with federal resources, broken down by document type, branch, and authoring institution, followed similarly by all states, the District of Columbia, and other United States jurisdictions; "T2: Foreign Jurisdictions," covering sources of law for dozens of countries across the world;[10] and "T6: Common Words in Case Names, Institutional Author Names, and Periodical Titles," particularly helpful when creating a citation to a secondary source not covered by the examples in the *Bluebook* or the *ALWD Guide.*

B. The *ALWD Guide*'s Greatest Hits

- Fast Formats

Similar to the Quick Reference guides in the *Bluebook*, the *ALWD Guide*'s Fast Formats offer at-a-glance examples of legal citations, for easy reference.

---

10. Rather than taking up a large amount of space in print, this table is available for free online at https://www.legalbluebook.com/bluebook/v21/tables/t2-foreign-jurisdictions.

Fast Formats are found at the beginning of each rule in the *ALWD Guide*, and contain examples for academic and non-academic publications alike.

- **Appendixes**

Similar to the Tables in the *Bluebook*, the *ALWD Guide* ends with a series of appendixes to further assist with your citation questions. You will see some overlap with the Tables in the *Bluebook*; for example, Appendix 1 provides a guide to the primary sources published by United States jurisdictions, similar to the *Bluebook's* table T1. But it is far from a 1:1 correlation. Appendix 6, for instance, covers federal tax materials specifically.

VI. Final Citation Tips

This appendix has focused on the most basic elements of legal citation, meant primarily to help you understand a citation when you come across it in your reading, but the *Bluebook* and the *ALWD Guide* cover far more, particularly if you are trying to format citations yourself. For information on parallel citations, the use of explanatory phrases and parentheticals and much, much more, refer to their storied pages.

Even if you become a legal citation expert, you will still often happen upon sources that you are unsure how to cite, sources not mentioned in either the *Bluebook* or the *ALWD Guide*. When this happens, there are a few steps you can take to set you on the right path, as depicted in Table A-6.

Table A-6. Formatting Difficult Citations

Recommended Steps	Considerations at Each Step	
1. Review the core elements and features of the source you intend to cite:	Ask yourself: What kind of document is this (statute, case, treatise, journal article, website)?	Based on the type of document, identify the most appropriate rule.
2. Once you identify the most likely rule, consider additional features of the document to help you identify the best examples in the *Bluebook* or *ALWD Guide* to follow, such as:	Who is the author? Is the publication multi-volume? How is the content organized? Where does my source start within the publication? What is the year of publication?	
3. When in doubt, always go back to the fundamental purpose of citations:	(1) Giving due credit to the source you are referencing (2) Providing sufficient information for your own readers to be able to locate the authority you are referencing	

If you keep those objectives in mind, identify the requisite elements your citation must include to satisfy those aims, and you choose the closest rule you can find in the *Bluebook* or the *ALWD Guide* to help you structure your citation, you have done your job.

Appendix B

Selected Bibliography of Indiana Legal Resources

The sources listed here are non-comprehensive, but comprise the most frequently consulted primary and secondary sources in Indiana law today. The intent of this appendix is to provide basic identification of the sources, with light annotation where appropriate. Many of these sources, particularly those listed under "Indiana Primary Sources," are discussed in greater detail in the chapters of this book.

Indiana Primary Sources

Case Law

North Eastern Reporter (First, Second, and Third Series)

The *North Eastern Reporter* has carried cases from the Indiana Supreme Court since 1885, the Indiana Court of Appeals since 1891, and the Indiana Tax Court since 1986. Today it is the official reporter for Indiana cases. Lower-level trial courts in Indiana do not publish written opinions.

Statutory Law

Indiana Code

Produced by the state, the *Indiana Code* is the official publication of codified statutes in Indiana. Thomson Reuters and LexisNexis each publish a commercial version of the *Indiana Code* as well, *West's Annotated Indiana Code* and *Burns Indiana Statutes Annotated*, respectively. Recall from Chapter 4 that annotated codes are helpful research references when conducting legal research, because they contain references to significant case law and secondary sources for researching a statute further.

Indiana Acts

Produced by the state, the Acts are a compilation of Indiana session laws, a chronological publication of all laws passed within a particular legislative session. This includes all public laws later codified in the *Indiana Code*, as well as private laws and other noncode acts.

Regulations

Indiana Administrative Code

Produced by the Indiana Legislative Services Agency, the *Indiana Administrative Code* is today the sole publication of codified regulations for the state of Indiana. A commercial, annotated version of the code was previously produced by Thomson Reuters, *West's Indiana Administrative Code*, but that title was discontinued in 2020. Today the *Indiana Administrative Code* is available in electronic format only.

Indiana Register

Produced by the Indiana Legislative Services Agency, the *Indiana Register*, a daily publication, publishes proposed and adopted regulations and other administrative notices. Unlike the *Indiana Administrative Code*, regulations in the *Indiana Register* are uncodified, arranged in each issue by agency, rather than by subject. The *Indiana Register* is available in electronic format only.

Indiana Secondary Sources

Encyclopedias, Treatises, and Practice Aids

Appellate Handbook for Indiana Lawyers (Matthew Bender)

Written specifically for Indiana attorneys, this practice aid provides detailed explanation and analysis of the Indiana Rules of Appellate Procedure, with guides to practice before the Indiana Supreme Court, Indiana Court of Appeals, and the Seventh Circuit Court of Appeals. Available in print and on Lexis.

Indiana Law Encyclopedia (Thomson West)

For short explanations of a broad array of legal topics in Indiana, the *Indiana Law Encyclopedia* is an excellent quick reference. Available in print and on Westlaw.

Indiana Model Civil Jury Instructions (Prepared by the Indiana Judges Association)

This practice aid provides an overview and commentary on the model Indiana civil jury instructions and can be a helpful tool for judges when providing instruction to juries; attorneys when proposing instructions to the court and when preparing a case; and researchers, in understanding civil matters in Indiana. Available in print and on Lexis or Westlaw.

Indiana Pattern Criminal Jury Instructions (Prepared by the Indiana Judges Association)

This practice aid provides sample jury instructions for criminal matters in Indiana, and includes an overview of relevant statutes and cases, commentary, and forms. Available in print and on Lexis or Westlaw.

Indiana Pleading & Practice with Forms (Matthew Bender)

This prominent practice aid dives deep into explanation and commentary on the Indiana Trial Rules and provides model forms for use in civil actions in Indiana. Available in print and on Lexis.

Indiana Practice Series (Thomson West)

Providing explanation and analysis of major areas of law in Indiana, including model legal forms, this practice aid is a prominent research tool for Indiana attorneys. Available in print and on Westlaw.

Midwest Transaction Guide (Matthew Bender)

Covering Illinois, Indiana, and Michigan, this practice aid provides a state by state overview and explanation of the law, focusing on business, wills and trusts, commercial, real estate, and personal transactions. Written for attorneys, this publication offers practical tips and guidance, as well as model forms for each state. Available in print and on Lexis.

Law Journals Produced by Indiana Law Schools

Indiana University Maurer School of Law

Indiana Journal of Constitutional Design, repository.law.indiana.edu/ijcd

Indiana Journal of Global Legal Studies, repository.law.indiana.edu/ijgls

Indiana Journal of Law & Social Equality, repository.law.indiana.edu/ijlse

Indiana Law Journal, repository.law.indiana.edu/ilj

IP Theory, repository.law.indiana.edu/ipt

Indiana University McKinney School of Law

Indiana Health Law Review, mckinneylaw.iu.edu/ihlr

Indiana International & Comparative Law Review, mckinneylaw.iu.edu/iiclr

Indiana Law Review, mckinneylaw.iu.edu/ilr

University of Notre Dame Law School

Notre Dame Journal of International & Comparative Law, ndjicl.org

Notre Dame Journal of Law, Ethics & Public Policy, jlepp.org

Notre Dame Journal of Legislation, ndjleg.com

Notre Dame Journal on Emerging Technologies, ndlsjet.com

Notre Dame Law Review, scholarship.law.nd.edu/ndlr

The American Journal of Jurisprudence, academic.oup.com/ajj

Bar Publications & Legal News

Indiana Lawyer, www.theindianalawyer.com

Produced by IBJ Media, the *Indiana Lawyer* is a bi-weekly print (and digital) publication covering legal news around the state.

Res Gestae

Res Gestae is a monthly publication of the Indiana State Bar Association. Its contents include articles, legal news, and ethics opinions in the state of Indiana. Available in print, on the Indiana State Bar Association website (for members), and on Lexis and Westlaw.

Indiana Government Websites

Indiana General Assembly, iga.in.gov

Provides access to the *Indiana Constitution*; the *Indiana Code*, 2009–present; *Indiana Acts*, 2000–present; bills and resolutions, 2000–present; *Indiana Register*, October 2000–present; *Indiana Administrative Code*, 2003–present; as well as drafting manuals, agency and fiscal reports, and other internal publications of the Indiana General Assembly.

Indiana Courts, in.gov/courts

Provides a variety of resources for interacting with the trial and appellate courts of Indiana. Notable features include a full-text database of recent opinions from the Indiana Supreme Court, Court of Appeals, and Tax Court, public.courts.in.gov/decisions?c=9510; and the Self-Service Legal Center, which provides guides and court forms for certain common legal issues related to family law, housing, employment, and small claims, in.gov/courts/selfservice/.

Additional Helpful Sources About Indiana

The following are a few more sources not specific to law that can be of help to attorneys and legal researchers in order to fully understand legal issues in Indiana.

Howey Politics Indiana, howeypolitics.com

Howey Politics has been a prominent source of political news in Indiana since 1994, covering politics and public policy in Indianapolis, Washington, D.C., and cities across the state. The Howey Politics website is a subscription-based source; but the site's founder, Brian Howey, donated copies of his publication, *The Howey Political Report*, to the Indiana State Library, where they can be accessed for free, with a 2-month embargo, in.gov/library/online-resources/howey-political-report/.

Indianapolis Business Journal (IBJ Media), ibj.com

Provides business and financial news for central Indiana and the Indianapolis metropolitan area. Available in print and digital subscription. Print publication is weekly.

Indiana GovInfo (INDIGO), indianagovinfo.org/blog-2

This blog from Indiana Networking for Documents and Information of Government Organizations (INDIGO), a special interest group of government information specialists around the state of Indiana, includes government information news and resources from both the state and federal government.

Indiana State Agency Databases (GODORT), godort.libguides.com/indianadbs

This guide from the American Library Association's Government Documents Roundtable provides an annotated list of links to searchable databases produced by Indiana state agencies, organized by subject.

Indiana Week in Review (WFYI), wfyi.org/programs/indiana-week-in-review

This weekly TV and radio program provides helpful insight and debate on the latest issues facing Indiana today, an informative resource for understanding the nuances of Indiana politics.

STATS Indiana, www.stats.indiana.edu

A preeminent and award-winning source for demographic and economic data in the state of Indiana, this site is intended for use across the spectrum, from government to education to business and nonprofits. Available through a partnership between Indiana University and the State Data Center Program at the Indiana State Library.

About the Authors

Ashley Ames Ahlbrand is the Associate Director for Public Services at the Jerome Hall Law Library, Indiana University Maurer School of Law. She regularly teaches a survey course in Advanced Legal Research as well as specialized Advanced Legal Research courses in tax and advocacy. Ashley is an active member of the Ohio Regional Association of Law Libraries (ORALL), where she currently serves as President; the Mid-America Association of Law Libraries (MAALL); and the American Association of Law Libraries (AALL), where she is a recent recipient of the 2021 Emerging Leader Award.

Ashley holds a B.A. from the College of William & Mary, a J.D. from the William & Mary Law School, and a M.L.S. from the Indiana University School of Library & Information Science.

Michelle Trumbo is the Assistant Director for the Legal Research, Writing, and Analysis Program at the Antonin Scalia Law School, George Mason University. Michelle returned to Scalia Law after a four-year stint as General Counsel for an automotive services company. Prior to her departure, she was Head of Reference and Instructional Services at George Mason's law library. Michelle is also the Executive Director of the Legal Information Preservation Alliance (LIPA).

Michelle holds a B.A. from the University of Maryland, a M.L.I.S. from the University of Washington, and a J.D. from Washington and Lee University.

Index

Appellee, 69

Articles, *see* Legal periodicals

Atlantic Reporter, 62

Attorney general opinions, 95, 109-110

Bar journals, 32, 34

Bill tracking

  Federal, 123

  Indiana, 116

Bills

  Federal, 120, 121, 122

  Indiana, 114, 116, 117, 118

Binding authority, *see* Mandatory authority

Blackford's Reports of Cases, 62

Bloomberg Law, 10, 11, 14, 17, 18, 19, 20, 30, 36, 37, 45, 53, 69, 70, 76, 80, 81, 82, 83, 84, 87, 88, 89, 90, 91, 92, 93, 99, 101, 107, 108

Bluebook, 59, 61, 64, 119

BNA, *see* Bureau of National Affairs

Boolean searching, *see* Terms-and-connectors searching

Brevier Legislative Reports, 9

Bureau of National Affairs (BNA), 36, 107, 108

Burns Indiana Statutes Annotated, 42, 45, 47

Case of first impression, 36

Case history, 93

  See also Procedural history

Case law research,

  Analysis, 72-74

  Citation, 63-64

Digests, 10, 78, 79, 80, 85

Headnotes, 70, 72, 75, 76, 78-79, 80, 85, 91

Reporters, 32, 55, 57, 61, 62, 63, 64-66, 69, 70, 78, 79, 80, 85

Research methods, 75-86

Updating, 88-89

CCH, *see* Commerce Clearinghouse

CCH Indiana State Tax Reporter, 32

Certiorari, 61

CFR, *see* Code of Federal Regulations

Citators,

  BCite (Bloomberg Law), 10, 14, 76, 81, 87, 88, 91, 92

  Cases, 76, 81, 87-93

  Generally, 7, 10, 11, 25, 87-93

  KeyCite (Westlaw), 10, 14, 25, 38, 50, 55, 76, 87, 88, 91, 92

  Law reviews and journals, 34

  Regulations, 100, 101, 106, 107

  Shepard's (Lexis), 10, 14, 25, 50, 55, 76, 80, 87, 88, 91, 92, 107

  Statutes, 49, 50, 75, 127

Cited decisions, *see* Table of Authorities

Citing References,

  Citing decisions, 42, 45, 76, 80, 81, 90-92, 93, 101

  Other citing sources, 45, 92

  Table of authorities (cited decisions), 28, 76, 81, 90, 92, 105

CJS, *see Corpus Juris Secundum*

CLE, *see* Continuing Legal Education

Primary sources, 4-8, 10-12, 17, 23, 25, 28, 41, 52, 75-76, 125, 127
Principles of the Law, 36-37
Private law, 122, 123
Procedural history, 89, 93
    See also Case history
Proclamations, 4, 23, 110, 123
Public law,
    Generally, 47, 51,115, 122, 123
    Public law number, 45, 115, 116, 122, 123

Regulations, 4-5, 7, 12, 14, 17, 23, 36, 45-48, 51, 75, 95-107, 110, 127
Remand, 73
Reporters,
    Advance sheets, 61
    Citation, 63-64, 69-70, 79, 84-85
    Federal cases, 65
    Indiana cases, 5, 77, 79, 82
    Regional reporters, 62-64
    Slip opinions, 61, 65
Res Gestae, 32-33
Research organization, 14, 21
Research process
    Administrative law, 95-111
    Bill tracking, 116, 123
    Cases, 75-85
    Citators, 14, 81, 87-93
    Constitutions, 41-43
    Legislative history, 113-124
    Organizing, 21, 127-128
    Planning, 13-16
    Secondary sources, 4-5, 7, 13-14, 23-24, 125-126
    Statutes, 45-48

Research strategies, 125-128
Research vocabulary, *see* Generating search terms
Respondent, 69, 73
Restatements of the Law, 36
Rulemaking
    Federal, 104
    Indiana, 97-98
Rules
    Administrative, 95-101, 104-107
    Court, 41, 52-55

Scope note, 24, 30, 35
Secondary sources,
    American Jurisprudence, 2d, 25, 27
    American Law Reports, 23-25, 27-28
    Bar journals, 32
    Continuing legal education, 30-31
    Corpus Juris Secundum, 25-26
    Encyclopedias, 7, 23-27, 34, 45, 125
    Forms, 27, 29-32, 55
    Generally, 23-39
    Jury instructions, 24, 31, 39
    Looseleaf services, 24, 36
    Periodicals, 32-34
    Persuasive authority, 4-5
    Practice guides, 27, 29
    Research process in, 7, 13-14, 23
    Restatements, 36-37
    Treatises, 7, 23, 27, 29, 34, 35-36, 55
    Uniform laws, 37-38